Isaac Shelby

A Driving Force in America's Struggle for Independence

By S. Roger Keller

Burd Street Press

Copyright © 2000 by S. Roger Keller

ALL RIGHTS RESERVED—No part of this book may be reproduced in any form without permission in writing from the publisher, except by a reviewer who wishes to quote brief passages in connection with a review.

This Burd Street Press publication
was printed by
Beidel Printing House, Inc.
63 West Burd Street
Shippensburg, PA 17257-0152 USA

In respect for the scholarship contained herein, the acid-free paper used in this book meets the guidelines for permanence and durability of the Committee on Production Guidelines for Book Longevity of the Council on Library Resources.

For a complete list of available publications
please write
Burd Street Press
Division of White Mane Publishing Company, Inc.
P.O. Box 152
Shippensburg, PA 17257-0152 USA

Library of Congress Cataloging-in-Publication Data

PRINTED IN THE UNITED STATES OF AMERICA

Contents

List of Illustrations			iv
Acknowledgments			v
Introduction			vi
Ballad of King's Mountain			xi
Chapter	1	Isaac Shelby	1
Chapter	2	Thicketty Fort	10
Chapter	3	Second Cedar Springs and Musgrove's Mill	13
Chapter	4	Going after Ferguson	23
Chapter	5	The Score Is Settled	31
Chapter	6	Away from the Mountain	47
Chapter	7	Other Duties	56
Chapter	8	Monck's Corner, November 1781; A Return to Farming	59
Chapter	9	Kentucky's First Governor	62
Chapter	10	The First Term	69
Chapter	11	Answering the Call as the Bloodletting Begins	73
Chapter	12	Shelby's Coming Through! Adventure in Canada	79
Chapter	13	Remembering the Raisin	85
Chapter	14	The Traveler Rests	91
Appendix A		"Backwater Men" Roster	96
Appendix B		A Letter to his Father, General Evan Shelby	104
Appendix C		The 1818 Treaty with the Chickasaw Indians	106
Bibliography			111
Index			114

iii

Illustrations

Isaac Shelby	2
Susannah Hart Shelby	3
John Murray, the fourth earl of Dunmore	5
Map of the region near Musgrove's Mill	16
Map of the battle of King's Mountain	33
Major Joseph Winston	39
Colonel John Sevier	42
Major Joseph McDowell	42
Lord Earl Cornwallis	43
President Herbert Hoover at King's Mountain	44
Death of Major Patrick Ferguson	44
Colonel Shelby's "Damned Yelling Boys"	45
First Kentucky State House	68
Second Kentucky State House	68
Map of the battle of the Thames	86
Tecumseh	87
William Henry Harrison	88
View of Traveler's Rest	95

iv

Acknowledgments

There are several people I wish to thank for assistance in completing this book.

First, Mrs. Peggy Arcidiacono, of Hagerstown, Maryland. Her invitation to speak to the Antietam Chapter of the Daughters of the American Revolution, of Washington County, Maryland, on the Revolutionary War sent me in search of a local hero. That hero was Isaac Shelby.

Additional thanks go to Cecil and Julia Wells, of Waynesboro, Pennsylvania. Mr. Wells grew up near King's Mountain, South Carolina, and its Revolutionary War battleground. His loan of writings by several historians of that area added greatly to the story.

Introduction

It was Thomas Jefferson who said it! King's Mountain was the "Joyful annunciation of the turn of the tide of success which terminated the Revolutionary War with the seal of Independence."

Certainly it can be said proudly, and without fear of contradiction, that Isaac Shelby, a native of Washington County, Maryland, was the instigator of this revolt against the oppressive British forces that had snuffed out all resistance in the southern United States by 1780. All opposition that is, except a rugged band of fearless mountain men, veterans of the savage Indian wars. They were fathers and grandfathers of future freedom fighters who would march with Andrew Jackson to overcome the Creeks and who provided Gen. Robert E. Lee and "Stonewall" Jackson with the best fighting men the world has yet seen.

The Battle of King's Mountain, in South Carolina, was more than a dramatic, unexpected victory by a ragtag, untrained army of farmers and mountain men. It was a turning point in our country's struggle for independence. It gave hope in the last hours as the enemy began a choking move to split the colonies, now known as states, into three parts and settle the war once and for all. It lit the light of freedom throughout the countryside and in the northern towns and villages. At last the British began to lose their stomach for fighting and in a few short months, the struggle was settled at Yorktown.

The American Revolution was a war that was almost lost. It can be said that the population of the 1700s was divided into thirds: one-third Loyalists, one-third Tory, and the other third uncommitted. And when push came to shove, the Loyalists showed up in greater numbers to fight for King George.

The Crown, in effect, overran Georgia and the Carolinas. It was by no means dominant, but with the appearance of the redcoats it came out in force. Most of the Scottish settlers sided with the Crown, just as in upstate New York where many small farmers remained Loyalists.

vi

Introduction vii

It is interesting to note that many Southern "backwoodsmen" and westerners had no love for the king, but considered themselves oppressed by the tidewater colonial assemblies by which they were underrepresented and often overtaxed. Oddly enough, parts of the South witnessed a revolution within a revolution when the eastern-dominated legislatures threw the royal government out, and the westerners rebelled and sided with the Crown. The divisions were blurred and turned the Southern campaign into a genuine civil war.

While the principal battles with the British professional armies occurred along the eastern seaboard, it continued afterwards in many ways on the frontiers and along the rims of America, long after Yorktown and the peace treaty with England was signed.

It can also be argued that the fight for independence may have been lost had not Britain been engaged in a world war. With the intervention of the French after 1778, the fighting extended from the West Indies to India placing England at times in danger of invasion as in the year of the Spanish Armada.

Then, after six years of blood, sweat, and tears, the Americans began to see that they were more than just soldiers of separate colonies. That through and because of their efforts a nation was born. In the words of South Carolina's Christopher Gadsden, uttered even before the fighting began, *"There ought to be no more New England men, no New Yorkers, but all of us Americans!"* The dream was about to become reality.

Interesting to Ponder

Military campaigns in the South during 1780 consisted mostly of partisan warfare fought over very wide areas. The armies were engaged only twice, at Charleston and Camden, South Carolina. Both were American disasters. The center of the American government at this time was Philadelphia, Pennsylvania. General Washington's headquarters during the first half of the year was at Morristown, New York. He was plagued with numerous problems: lack of supplies, a devaluated currency, starving soldiers, and a wavering support from the ranks. In a letter to Baron von Steuben in April, Washington hoped for an extrication from the situation in the near future, while indicating unbound faith in the "cause."

The British ruled the ocean, holding the ports of Penobscot, Halifax, New York, Charleston, and Savannah. Washington noted that it was their (the British) fault that the feeble manner in which they had applied their means at hand that the colonies had not suffered more. The French would be essential to achieve independence and he was counting on General Marie-Joseph La Fayette to return from France with good news. Washington and the nation's prayers were answered on April 27 when La Fayette returned with the joyous news that the French fleet and army would follow very soon. Washington and the Congress drew a deep sigh of relief.

Introduction

The dark clouds on the horizon were beginning to yield to a few, thin rays of sunshine.

The "backwater" or "over-the-mountain" men of western North Carolina knew very little of the war. They were satisfied with their seclusion in the valleys of the Holston, the Watauga and the Nolachucky. Here, they found full freedom to practice their religion and raise their families.

It is probable that had Lord Earl Cornwallis ignored the western Carolinas and confined his army's sweep north to the eastern plains and lowlands, the mountain men would have remained at home; had not Major (later lieutenant colonel) Patrick Ferguson uttered his threat of fire and sword and the hangman's noose, these uncommon men would not have become involved.

As so often happens in the course of history, hindsight looks at both events and judges from afar. The British committed a major blunder when they taunted these raw, indefatigable Indian fighters *and it changed the war and course of American history.*

Getting Its Name

King's Mountain is the second largest town in Cleveland County, South Carolina. It began as White Plains. Upon the completion of the Charlotte to Atlanta airline railway in 1872, some of the engineering crew at the home of Dr. and Mrs. James Wright Tracey asked Mrs. Tracey to select a new name for the permanent town. The post office was kept in the Tracey home at that time and she determined the infant town's new name would be King's Mountain, in honor of the pivotal Revolutionary War battle that was fought there, and in honor of the brave Patriots who killed Colonel Ferguson.

Prior to the Revolutionary War that area was settled by the Scotch-Irish and the Pennsylvania Dutch.

A SHORT CHRONOLOGY OF THE WAR FOR INDEPENDENCE

1765
The Stamp Act riots. The act is repealed.

1770
The Boston Massacre.

1771
The Regulator movement is crushed in North Carolina.

1773
Parliament passes the "Tea Act."
The Boston Tea Party.

Introduction

1774
At Point Pleasant, the "backwater" men, led by the Shelbys, prove to the Shawnees that they have come of age as fighters.
The First Continental Congress meets in Philadelphia, Pennsylvania.

1775
The Cherokees sell Kentucky and the lands along the Watauga to Judge Henderson at a big gathering along the river.
Minutemen assemble to warn citizens of the British advance on Lexington and Concord.
The Continental Congress authorizes the formation of a Continental army.
General George Washington is named commander in chief.
The Battle of Bunker (Breed's) Hill. British occupy Boston.
The British and the Americans get their noses bloodied by the French and the Indians at the Battle of the Monongahela.
The "Green Mountain Boys" win the Battle of Crown Point.

1776
Patriots pull down a statue of King George III in New York.
Thomas Paine publishes "Common Sense."
Defeat at Quebec City, Canada.
France and Spain lend aid to the American cause, thus broadening the war for the British.
Congress changes the country's name from United Colonies of America, to United States of America. The Declaration of Independence is signed.
Battles around New York. Americans lose at Long Island, Harlem Heights, and White Plains.
The Watauga men defeat the Cherokees at Island Flats as war rages along the frontier.
In September, three states combine to raid and ravage the Cherokee Nation.
On Christmas Day, Washington launches the attack on Trenton, New Jersey.

1777
Victory at Princeton and Saratoga. British capture Ticonderoga.
France allies with America. Burgoyne surrenders entire army to Americans.
Americans lose at Brandywine. Valley Forge.

1778
France recognizes American Independence.
The British navy bombards and raids coastal cities.
Battle of Monmouth: British retire under cover of night.

1779
War reaches a standoff in the North.
The British occupy New York City, and move their concentration of power to the South. They continue raids and attacks on coastal towns.
John Paul Jones captures man-of-war near English coast.

Introduction

1780

The British attack Charleston, South Carolina and the only
Continental army in the South surrenders.
Patriots are slaughtered at Waxhaws and the
war cry "Tarleton's quarter" is born.
Patriots defeat Tories at Ramseur's Mill.
Isaac Shelby wins the Battle of Fort Thicketty.
Major Patrick Ferguson invades North Carolina.
The "backwater" men, led by **Isaac Shelby,** rally at
Sycamore Shoals and vow to "git" Ferguson.
On October 7, Ferguson is soundly defeated and killed at King's Mountain,
and all of his men (all were Americans) are either killed or captured.
Rochambeau arrives in America with 5,500 men.

1781

The British fleet appears with an army on board.
The British are defeated at Cowpens and Guilford Court House.
Lord Earl Cornwallis surrenders at Yorktown.
General Nathanael Greene clears South Carolina and Georgia of the enemy.

1782

George Rogers Clark defeats British-supported Indians in the West.
Provisional Peace.

1783

Treaty of Peace at Paris.

Ballad of King's Mountain

Ferguson's Defeat

Come all you good people, I pray you draw near.
A tragical story you quickly shall hear
of Whigs and Tories, how they bred a great strife,
When they chased old Ferguson out of his life.

Brave Colonel Williams from Hillsboro came,
The South Carolinians flocked to him again,
Four hundred and fifty, a jolly brisk crew,
After old Ferguson we then did pursue.

We march'd to Cowpens—Brave Campbell was there,
And Shelby, and Cleveland, and Colonel Sevier,
Taking the lead of their bold mountaineers,
Brave Indian fighters devoid of all fears.

Like eagles a hungry in search of their prey,
We chased the old fox the best part of the day,
At length on King's Mountain the old rogue we found,
And we, like old heroes, his camp did surround.

The battle did last the best part of an hour,
The guns they did roar—the bullets did shower,
With an oath in our hearts to conquer the field,
We rushed to the Tories, resolv'd they should yield.

We laid old Ferguson dead on the ground,
Four hundred and fifty dead Tories lay around,
Making a large escort, it not quite so wise,
To guide him to his chosen abode in the skies.

We shouted the victory that we did obtain,
Our voices were heard seven miles on the plain,
Liberty shall stand—and the Tories shall fall,
Here's an end to my song, so God bless us all.

Author unknown.

xi

Chapter One

☆☆☆☆☆☆☆☆☆☆☆☆☆☆☆

Isaac Shelby

Isaac Shelby was born in what is today Washington County, Maryland, near the small village of Clear Spring, on December 11, 1750. His father was Evan Shelby, Jr., the son of Evan Shelby, Sr., an early settler in the vast woodlands of the county, and a rugged, old Indian fighter and fur trapper who emigrated from Wales in 1720. At one time the senior Shelby owned large tracts of land bordered by the ancient Potomac River on the south and extending north into Pennsylvania.

Shelby established a fort on a plot of land known as Maiden's Choice. Along with several other forts strung out between the Mason-Dixon Line on the north, and the Potomac to the south and extending westward, each fort offered protection to travelers and settlers from occasional Indian attacks.

In August 1744, Isaac's father married Letitia Cox, of Fredericktown, Maryland (Frederick, today). The union produced five sons, Isaac being the second, and two daughters.

When young Isaac was about five years old, Maryland Governor Horatio Sharp directed the building of a large stone fort (Fort Frederick) along the Potomac River, only a few miles from the Shelby homeplace for further protection insurance. General Henry Bouquet wrote that the Shelby fort was located six miles from Fort Frederick.

The senior Shelby died in 1756, when his grandson was less than six years old.

In 1758 Maryland troops volunteered for an offensive move against Fort Duquesne. Issac's father, now a captain, was given the difficult task of surveying a road between Fort Frederick and Fort Cumberland. It extended through sixty miles of thick, stubborn forest and over seven mountains. A portion of that same road can be traveled today as U.S. Route 40. Eventually the French abandoned Fort Duquesne and it was renamed Fort Pitt.

Growing up in the woods of western Maryland, young Isaac took rapidly to survival abilities and became an expert woodsman, learning

Mezzotint of Isaac Shelby after portrait by Matthew Harris Jouett, Kentucky's first resident portrait painter

Isaac Shelby, Kentucky's First Governor

Susannah Hart Shelby

Courtesy Mrs. Eleanor Tevis Faulconer. Copied by Jack Coleman.

Chapter One

most of his skills from his father. His formal education lasted a short two years. In his late teens he served briefly as the sheriff of Fredericktown, Maryland. (Note: Present day Washington County was originally Prince Georges County until 1748 when it became Frederick County as the state began to fragment. In 1776, in the middle of the Revolutionary War, Washington County broke away taking with it present day Allegheny and Garrett Counties which, in turn, were formed in later years.)

Young Shelby was active along the Maryland and Pennsylvania borders during the French and Indian War. On one occasion he discovered an Indian spy, chased him a great distance, and in front of many of his troops overtook him and proceeded to administer the tomahawk to the head of the enemy.

When not pursuing the Indians, he raised and fed cattle on the family's vast holdings west of the Alleghenies.

During the Pontiac uprising in 1763 the Shelby's fur trading business was ruined by the Indians, and in the same year his homeplace was destroyed by fire, plunging the family deep into debt.

In the summer of 1765, as the Shelbys debated moving south to start anew, they received visitors. Charles Mason and Jeremiah Dixon presented themselves at their rebuilt home and explained that they were surveying a line to divide Maryland from Pennsylvania. They requested Isaac's father to accompany them to the top of North Mountain to reveal to them the course of the "Potowmack" (Potomac) River westward toward the "Conoloways," (Tonoloways). This would be a point where the Mason-Dixon line nearly severs the western "neck" of Maryland. A few days later, after spending a pleasant visit with the Shelbys, and manufacturing a number of the markers to be set in place dividing the two states, the party moved on westward. (One of the markers, considered to be imperfect, may be seen today in the barn on the senior Shelby's homeplace. It is located along Broadfording Road, east of Clear Spring, Maryland, and is owned by Mr. and Mrs. Charles Downs.)

Early in the 1760s, Isaac's father negotiated a treaty with the Indians, giving him a vast amount of land that included all of the present state of West Virginia lying between the Ohio, Little Kanawha and the Monongahela Rivers. In 1771, along with a neighbor friend, Isaac Baker (after whom Isaac was named), they relocated to the Holston River area in what was at that time believed to be Virginia. However, a later resurvey showed the area to be in North Carolina. Today, it is in Tennessee. They purchased the Sapling Grove tract of land, amounting to 1,946 acres, and divided it equally among themselves. There, the families settled to raise cattle. The Shelbys opened and operated a very successful general store catering to families moving westward. At Sapling Grove, Isaac helped build a sturdy log home on land that would later become the present-day twin cities of Bristol, Virginia and Bristol, Tennessee.

The Old Dominion had a tradition of quarreling with the mother country and royal officials that was a century old. In 1676 Nathaniel Bacon inspired a revolt against its aging Governor Sir William Berkeley in a heated disagreement about Indian policy. The following confrontation resulted in the burning of Jamestown, the capital, and 1,000 royal troops being sent to restore order. So demanding were the Virginians about being denied their rights at the turn of the century that they refused to use the royal mail, that required high fees as a form of tax. Virginians had also been leaders in opposition to the Stamp Act in 1765.

That same year Patrick Henry delivered a speech that reverberated throughout Virginia and the colonies. "Caesar," he cried, "has his Brutus, Charles the First his Cromwell, and George the Third may profit by their example!" However, moderates and conservatives rebuked Henry on the spot.

The royal governor of Virginia, John Murray, the fourth earl of Dunmore, chose to ignore the events of recent history and could see nothing on the immediate horizon other than a full-blown revolution, even though, at this point in time, none existed. He had almost started a war between Pennsylvania and Virginia about ownership of thousands of acres of land along the Ohio River. A royal proclamation of 1763 prohibited British settlements west of the Appalachians but Dunmore ignored it and provoked a war with the Shawnees by circulating a proclamation throughout the upper Ohio Valley that the colonists and the Shawnees were already engaged in war. Despite assurances from moderate Indian leaders that they would not wage war, the situation became increasingly tenuous as white settlers killed many Indians, inviting retaliation.

As the Shawnees fought to block settlement in this area, Lord Dunmore called forth an army and waged war. All of this came to a head in the fall of 1774 at Point Pleasant (now West Virginia), at the junction of the Kanawha and Ohio Rivers.

John Murray, the fourth earl of Dunmore, and the royal governor of Virginia

He precipitated a war against the Ohio Indians led by Chief Cornplanter at the Battle of Point Pleasant (now West Virginia). Isaac Shelby served in his father's company from Fincastle County, Virginia in the victory over the Indians.

Year of Illusion-1776

Chapter One

Persistent Indian atrocities along the Ohio River enraged the settlers and aroused the men to action. Isaac received a commission as a lieutenant in the command of Colonel William Preston, of Fincastle County, Virginia, with the goal of seeking out and defeating these various tribes. Isaac possessed a massive build and an imposing appearance. He had deep-set eyes, a strong mouth and chin, heavy eyebrows, uncommon intelligence, courage, and unquestioned integrity.

Efforts to assemble forces sufficient to deal with the Indians were successful with volunteers also being recruited from Augusta, Bottetourt, Frederick, Shenandoah and other Virginia counties—about twenty-five hundred in all.

All along the line of march to the field of battle, designated as a point on the Ohio River, Indian scouts kept track of the troop movements, sending reports daily to Cornstalk, chief of the Shawnees. Initially, the wise chief had opposed a war against the white man, but many other chiefs, who were also cautious in such matters, were shouted down by the more violent leaders, and Cornstalk gave in to their demands.

At Point Pleasant, on October 10, 1774, the frontier riflemen joined together to fight the allied Indian tribes (referred to as Lord Dunmore's War). Isaac was second in command of his father's company and served with great bravery. And, for the first time an American-supplied, -officered and -commanded army defeated an Indian army of about the same size and strength.

Advancing to the field to participate in the fight was a company of riflemen from Maryland under Captain Michael Cresap who was ordered to the rear of Dunmore's slow-moving column. Cresap, a renowned Indian fighter and the first captain named by Maryland in the Revolutionary War, was enraged. Dunmore was known to greatly respect Cresap's ability to fight and reasoned that if his men were attacked by the Indians from the front and fell back on Cresap, he would rally them and make a successful advance. Once so informed of Dunmore's reasoning, Captain Cresap and his men were satisfied.

Colonel Andrew Lewis, of Culpeper County, made camp on the eighth with 800 men. Point Pleasant was situated on a peninsula of land bounded by the Ohio River on the west, on the south by the New River, and on the east by a creek.

A small party of his men left the camp on the morning of the tenth not being aware that during the night a war party from the united tribes of Shawnee, Delaware, Mingoes, Taways, and several others had crossed the Ohio on 70 rafts.

Three miles along a trail the men were attacked by a large party of Indians and chased into camp. This precipitated what has been described as the largest and most savage battle between Indian and white man in the eastern colonies.

Captain Michael Cresap

Captain Michael Cresap returned to Maryland, and in the spring of 1775 he went to Ohio where he had been engaged previously in improving the lands along the Ohio River. On returning to his home later, near Cumberland, Maryland, he learned of the fighting at Lexington and the shedding of American blood. Committees were formed and companies were raised for defense. The committee of Frederick County, Maryland, encompassing present-day Washington, Allegheny, and Garrett Counties as a part, was ordered to raise two companies of riflemen. Cresap, along with Thomas Price, of Fredericktown, were immediately named captains. Despite being in poor health, Cresap answered his country's call and sent word for his company to form again. Twenty-two of the deadliest sharpshooters turned out with their own arms and equipment, ready and fully dedicated to go to the defense of their new country. They marched first to Fredericktown, a distance of one hundred miles, then proceeded from there with the other company and volunteers to Boston, joining the American army under General George Washington. However, Cresap's health began to fail. He began the long return journey home and died as he reached New York City, at the age of thirty-three years.

During the fighting Colonel John Fields, of Virginia, a veteran of the French and Indian War, was killed, and command fell to Captain Evan Shelby, Isaac's father.

Throughout the afternoon, attack after attack by the Indians was repulsed leading to their frustration. It had been much harder than they expected. Gradually, the Indians broke off the engagement and afterwards made desperate efforts at carrying away their dead and wounded. Shelby's men shot many of these and by day's end, Shelby said, "The field belongs to us!" The Indians scalped many of their own dead to prevent them from falling into the "white devil's" hands! They also buried many and threw several into the Ohio River. The victors took 18 scalps, most of them Shawnee. On the twelfth the scalps of the enemy were dressed and hung on a pole near the riverbank, and plunder was collected, including guns, blankets, tomahawks and powder horns.

The army losses were calculated at about seventy-five killed and one hundred and fifty wounded. As news of the victory by the frontiersmen spread from the valley, the effect was electric on American confidence.

With the defeat of Cornstalk and his tribes, Point Pleasant was made into a garrison where young Shelby remained in service until July 1775.

Chapter One

Then, Lord Dunmore, the English governor, ordered the troops disbanded, fearing they might enlist their sympathies with and become obedient to the Whig authorities.

After their sound defeat at the hands of the white men, and destruction of their villages, the various Indian tribes grudgingly accepted Cornstalk's peaceful methods for living with the "long rifles."

In 1776, Henderson and Company purchased large tracts of land from the Cherokees, in what is today Kentucky. They proceeded to hire Isaac Shelby to survey the thick forests and woodlands, for which he was commissioned a captain.

In July of the same year George Rogers Clark called a meeting at Jim Harrod's farm to discuss the purchase which he considered illegal. The land was intended to form a new *country* to be named Transylvania. Clark argued that the idea was interesting, but how could a new country defend itself? It would need an armed force to do that and to repel the continuous Indian attacks. As there was not even enough powder for the guns that were present for the meeting, they must ask for help from Virginia. The plan was to ask Virginia to make a section of Fincastle County the county of Kentucky, with its own delegates to the Virginia General Assembly. Then, it would have a right to demand, and get, much needed military aid.

A petition was drawn up asking the Virginia government for recognition, designating Clark and attorney John Jones as representatives. The petition was signed by the leading representatives of the various settlements, including Simon Kenton, Isaac Shelby, Daniel Boone, and his brother Squire Boone, Joseph Crockett, Benjamin Logan, and Simon Butler.

In 1777, Governor Patrick Henry appointed Isaac Shelby a commissary of supplies for a large number of militia, stationed at several frontier garrisons, to guard the back settlements and to lay in supplies for a grand treaty, to be held at the Long Island of the Holston River with the Cherokee Indians. Young Shelby displayed a tireless energy in making deliveries and obtaining supplies for the frontiersmen. He covered huge distances in short periods of time. In 1778 he continued his duties by supplying the army that battled the Ohio Indians. In the same year, a number of volunteers served under Shelby at a garrison, Fort Shelby, along Beaver Creek above the north fork of the Holston River, near the line between Virginia and eastern Tennessee. Samuel Riggs in his pension application dated 4 April 1834, says, "There were no Continental troops. There were about thirty men under Captain Isaac Shelby...engaged the greater part of the time in keeping the fort. The fort was capable of containing five hundred people. Captain Shelby's company was constantly in service, in doing duties as sentries, or in scouting parties and in all such service as was necessary for the protection of the families of the frontier settlement." (Riggs served beginning in July 1778 for three months.)

Isaac Shelby

Then, in 1779, Isaac pledged his individual credit to his father's troops while on the Chickamauga expedition. During this period he was elected to the Virginia legislature from Washington County. Shortly afterwards Governor Thomas Jefferson commissioned him a major for the escort of guards to the commissioners. They were engaged in extending the boundary line between Virginia and North Carolina. The new survey put Major Shelby's residence in North Carolina. Due to this, Isaac was appointed a colonel and magistrate of the new county of Sullivan, by North Carolina Governor Richard Caswell.

In the spring and early summer of 1780, Colonel Shelby was overseeing land interests in Kentucky which five years earlier he had marked and claimed for himself. At this time the fall of Charleston was announced which greatly alarmed him and caused his immediate return to home in July. He was determined to enter and remain in the service until liberty had been attained for his country. On his arrival he found an urgent message from Col. Charles McDowell, of Burke County, begging Shelby to furnish all of the aid he could towards checking the enemy. The enemy was overrunning the Southern states and had reached the western borders of North Carolina. Shelby responded immediately, crossing the Alleghenies with 200-mounted riflemen.

As Shelby advanced into North Carolina, Colonel McDowell, with 300 men, had pushed on toward the overrun territory. He made camp on July 15 at Earl's Ford on the North Pacolet River where he was surprised by British Major Dunlap, and suffered heavy losses. The severity of the situation immediately became apparent. McDowell began to organize a plan for reinforcements, and began recruiting efforts among the sparsely populated settlements on the headwaters of the Catawba, Broad, and Pacolet Rivers. Patrols were sent out to watch the enemy's movements; the British were roaming about the countryside, pillaging and marauding without the slightest impunity.

McDowell dashed off urgent messages to Isaac Shelby and Colonel John Sevier to come to his aid. In a very short time after the battle at Earl's Ford, Colonel McDowell took post on Broad River in what is now Cherokee County. Shelby joined him on July 25 with his contingent of 200 men. Col. Elijah Clarke, with his Georgians, accompanied by backwoodsmen who resided west of the Broad River, and who wished to resist the British, retired to that quarter. Capt. William Smith, of the Spartan district, with his company of Indian fighters also joined with Clarke, McDowell, Shelby, Sevier, and Andrew Hampton.

Chapter Two

☆☆☆☆☆☆☆☆☆☆☆☆☆☆☆☆

Thicketty Fort

Colonel McDowell and his refurbished troops refused to remain idle at the Cherokee Ford. On the evening of July 29, 1780, six hundred men were dispatched under Colonels Shelby, Clarke, and Hampton and Major Charles Robertson to conduct a surprise raid on Fort Thicketty, or Fort Anderson. The fort was located in an opening surrounded by thick woods north of the small meandering Goucher Creek. It had been built years earlier as a defense against repeated Cherokee Indian raids and was surrounded by an abatis making it a rather formidable bastion.

By daybreak of the thirtieth the Patriots had surrounded the old fort. Shelby sent Captain William Cocke to demand an immediate surrender of the bastion. The fort was under the command of the famous Tory leader Patrick Moore who vowed he would defend it to the last extremity.

Moore's men had made frequent raids into the countryside, plundering the homes of numerous Whig families. On one occasion a group visited the home of Patriot Captain Nathanael Jeffries, stole all the food, clothing and other items that they wanted, abused Mrs. Jeffries, and then drove off all of the family's horses and cattle.

On another occasion Moore's raiders met with Patriot resistance at the home of Miss Nancy Jackson, who resided in an Irish settlement near Fair Forest Creek. One of his men pursued the woman to the upstairs level only to have her spin around and kick him down the stairs. In his anger he threatened to send the Hessian troops to her home to teach her a lesson. Miss Jackson was obliged to leave her home and seek safety with relatives several miles away.

Knowing of the outrages committed by the fort's occupants and not wanting to waste any time in making amends, Shelby and Clarke immediately made their lines easily visible to the defenders, giving the impression that a full-scale assault was imminent. The six hundred men presented a rather formidable foe to Moore.

Thicketty Fort

Shelby sent Cocke, a volunteer and former United States senator from Tennessee, to the fort under a white flag. As Shelby and Clarke urged their men to make loud noises and brandish their arms, Cocke demanded an immediate surrender of the fort and its arms to which Moore yelled back from behind its wall that he would defend to the death! Immediately, Shelby tightened his lines to within easy musket shot of the fort and increased the volume of yelling and shouting. Horses pranced about in readiness for the order to charge the bastion. Apparently the "show" made such an impression on Moore that he had second thoughts and capitulated. His demands that his garrison be paroled, never to serve again in the war, were accepted.

Shelby would not have to be encumbered with the ninety-three Loyalists and one British sergeant-major who surrendered without firing a shot. The Patriots entered the fort and claimed two hundred and fifty stands of arms all loaded with musket ball and buckshot.

The jubilant Patriots celebrated the fall of the fort which relieved much suffering. The next day, loaded down with their spoils, they returned to McDowell's camp at the Cherokee Ford.

Later Patriot accounts tell that among the trophies taken from King's Mountain was the fragment of a letter, without date or signature, describing the capture of Fort Thicketty. "It had an upper line of loop-holes [much like those you see today in the sides of nineteenth-century barns. The holes are about three to four feet high and two to three inches wide, wider on the inside than on the outside, aiding in circulating air, and the drying of wheat and hay etc.] and was surrounded by a very strong abatis, [an ancient fortification consisting of sharpened tree branches pointing outward from a defensive position] with only a small wicket to enter by. It had been put through repair at the request of the garrison, which consisted of the neighboring militia that had come to the fort, and was defended by eighty men, against two to three hundred banditti without cannon, and each man was of the opinion that it was impossible for the Rebels to take it. The officer next in command and all the others gave their opinion for defending it and agreed in their account that Patrick Moore, after proposing a surrender, acquiesced in their opinion and offered to go and signify as much to the Rebels, but returned with some Rebel officers, whom he put in possession of the gate and the place, and who were instantly followed by their men and the fort full of Rebels, to the surprise of the garrison. He pleaded cowardice, I understand."

In a post-war account left by Patriot Lyman C. Draper he offers the following description of Patrick Moore: "He was of Irish descent and a native of Virginia. He early settled on Thicketty Creek in the northwestern part of South Carolina, where he commanded Fort Anderson, or Fort Thicketty, which he surrendered without firing a gun, to Col. Shelby and associates. He was subsequently captured by a party of Americans, according to tradition in his family, near Ninety-Six, and was supposed to have been killed by his captors, as his remains were afterwards found and recognized by his great height—six feet and seven inches tall. His death probably occurred in 1781. He left a widow who survived many years, a son and three daughters; and his descendants in South Carolina and Georgia are very worthy people."

Chapter Three

☆☆☆☆☆☆☆☆☆☆☆☆☆☆☆

Second Cedar Springs and Musgrove's Mill

After the capture of Fort Thicketty, McDowell's force numbered no more than a thousand men. His main British threat, Major Patrick Ferguson, was believed to have under his command about eighteen hundred men. The Patriots were thus resigned to maintaining their position at the ford, guarding against a surprise attack. That was entirely possible since a large number of the homes in that area were supporters of King George III. The Patriot leaders set about on a systematic routine of attacks on detached portions of the enemy as the opportunities became available. To better accomplish this mission McDowell detached six hundred mounted men, under Colonels Shelby, Clarke, and William Graham, to advance toward Ferguson's post located in the Fair Forest section of what is today Union County, South Carolina. Orders were to watch the movement of Ferguson's men and, whenever possible, to cut off and capture his foraging parties. The small army moved downstream about twenty-five miles in the general direction of Brown's Creek. Reaching a point on Brown's Creek, considered a good post for observing Ferguson's men, they came suddenly upon a far superior force of the enemy. Shelby suggested circling around the enemy. Successfully, they rode off to the northwest bringing them to Forest Creek on the evening of the seventh of August. Shelby and Clarke halted for refreshments at or near the present Foster's Mill, in what is today Spartanburg County. But, the stop was abruptly ended as Ferguson had dispatched Major Dunlap with a contingent to cut short this adventure by the upstart Americans.

During the night several of Shelby's scouts reported that the enemy was within a half mile. A stroke of good luck occurred for the Patriots when, as the scouts were finishing their report, a gunshot was heard in the distance, coming from the direction of the British soldiers. It was later determined that it was fired by one of Dunlap's men who may have had misgivings about the idea of surprising and massacring his own countrymen.

13

Chapter Three

Shelby sounded the alert and in minutes his troops marched away from the site, moving in the direction of Cedar Springs. When Dunlap arrived and observed the remains of the just-deserted camp, he cursed at the missed opportunity and ordered his men to rest. The pursuit would continue at first light.

Anticipating that they would be followed, and quickly, Shelby and Clarke selected a line of battle on the crest of a long hill to the northwest of the spring. This had barely been completed before spies came running into camp reporting that the enemy's horses were almost in sight. Both sides were eager to fight; the British being overconfident rushed forward as if the battle had already been decided.

It was mid-morning as Dunlap's men made their advance, finding the Americans in a good defensive position and apparently ready for a fight. The attack was led by his mounted riflemen. His men charged the Patriot line and as was expected met with a hot sheet of flame and musket balls that repelled the advance. Shelby and Clarke directed their men to pick off the horsemen which they did with amazing accuracy. There were several efforts made at breaking the Patriot line but none succeeded. Dunlap, realizing that he had jumped into a real mess, quickly ordered a retreat. The Patriots pursued the fleeing Whigs about two miles. Dunlap met Ferguson's force advancing against Shelby and Clarke. At this development the Patriot officers ordered a retreat, halting several times on favorable ground to fire at the enemy's advance until they reached the vicinity of the old iron works.

Several of the wounded were left behind and were properly cared for by Ferguson. Shelby and Clarke's men together had captured about fifty of the enemy, mostly British, including officers. Ferguson made several attempts at freeing his men but was not successful. He continued to find stubborn resistance to his advances as the American leaders would form on the most advantageous ground to give battle, then disappear only to reappear elsewhere on another advantageous position.

During the most severe part of the battle the brave actions of Colonel Clarke caught Shelby's attention. Clarke maintained a cool presence during hand-to-hand combat despite receiving two saber wounds. One was to the back of the neck and the other on his head, his stock buckle saving his life. And for a few minutes he was a prisoner in the hands of two husky Britons, but having confidence in his own strength, he knocked one of them down while the other fled. Colonel Clarke's son was also wounded.

The running fight continued on to Wofford's Iron Works and beyond, to near Cedar Springs. The hardest fighting occurred at the midpoint allowing for some to name the engagement the Second Battle of Cedar Springs and by others the Battle of Wofford's Iron Works. Ferguson followed the retreating Americans to the Pacolet River, or present day Clifton Mill No. 1. (It is often referred to as Glendale or by its much older name of

Second Cedar Springs and Musgrove's Mill   15

Bibingsville, three miles east of Cedar Springs.) At this point he gave up the chase. Shelby and Clarke, not having a base of operations or a fixed camp, were too elusive for the British-led Loyalists to catch.

Near the river the two American officers took position on a steep, rocky hill, fifty to sixty feet high. The road passes were so steep that the men, in some instances, had to help their horses up the steep ascent. As Ferguson and his men came into view they immediately determined a charge would mean suicide for all, and promptly turned away. The Patriots, from the safety of their high ground, bantered and ridiculed the enemy to their heart's content. Ferguson, having maintained the chase for more than five miles, withdrew with nothing to boast about except his superior numbers.

The Battle of Silver Springs is also referred to in this rural section of South Carolina as the "Battle of the Peach Orchard." The fruit trees were said to be thick on the grounds at that time. Some later accounts say most of the initial fighting started in a peach orchard when Patriot scouts fired on Dunlap's scouts who were picking peaches at the time.

Whig losses were estimated at four killed and twenty wounded. British losses were reported approximately twenty and thirty killed and wounded.

Before Clarke and Shelby left their camp on Fair Forest, Joseph Culbertson, who has been described as one of the bravest of young men, obtained permission to visit his family only two to three miles away. His objective was to make observations and gain valuable information that would be of use to the Patriots. Early the next morning he rode fearlessly into the camp that he had left the day before, assuming that it was still occupied by his friends. However, Shelby and Clarke had decamped and Dunlap had taken possession of the ground. Discovering his mistake, he casually rode out again and when out of sight spurred his mount forward to advise the Patriot leaders. As he passed through the camp he noticed that the dragoons were getting their horses ready to move out and renew their line of march. Eventually, he overtook Shelby and Clarke and found they had made preparations in anticipation of an attack.

Battle of the Peach Orchard

Local historians explain that as late as 1842 there were as many as twenty grave sites of the dead who fought in the battle, near a stone wall on the battlefield. And that after the war the widow of a Tory came to the place and had all of the bodies disinterred, from which she selected the remains of her husband, who was six feet, six inches tall. These she carried off for a burial elsewhere.

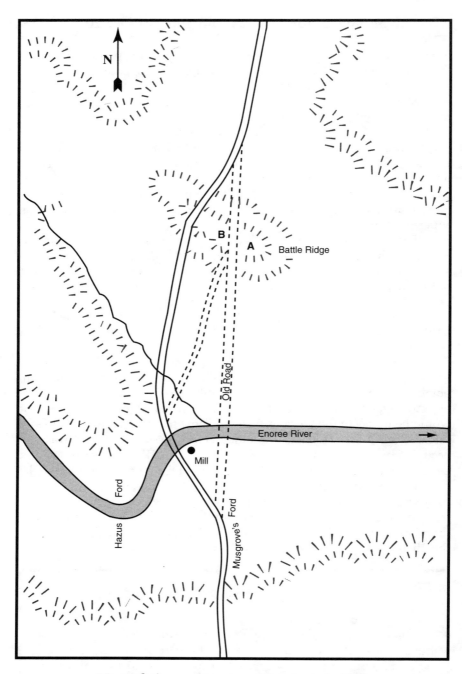

Map of the region near Musgrove's Mill

(A) Graves. (B) Location where Captain Inman was killed, at the junction of the old and new roads.

King's Mountain

Second Cedar Springs and Musgrove's Mill   17

The Americans staggered into McDowell's camp in great need of rest and food, having been without for several days. They had a short time to "catch up" before McDowell moved his camp from the ford to the east bank of the river at Smith's Ford, about ten miles distant. Shelby remained anxious to continue striking out at the enemy, especially at this time since enlistments of many of his men were about to expire. He yearned for more action before returning to his home on the Holston.

Colonel McDowell remained vigilant and learned from his numerous scouts that Ferguson was at Fair Forest, in the Brandon settlement, about twenty-six miles from his encampment. When the command of Colonel James Williams arrived in camp he further learned from Williams that some 200 Loyalists were in camp at Musgrove's Mill, guarding a rocky ford on the Enoree River, about forty miles from Smith's Ford and some fourteen miles southwest of Ferguson's camp.

McDowell reasoned that to attack the Loyalists would be the preferred move. They were less trained and disciplined than Ferguson's forces, that were made up of some very good fighting material. Secondly, if the Loyalists could be beaten it would open the way to Fort Ninety-Six, where a British garrison was stationed and which might be stormed and captured. Also, there was a rumor that a large British war chest was moving along the same road.

Immediately, McDowell dispatched his two warriors, Shelby and Clarke, to go with Williams and attack them. The men were all volunteers from Colonel McDowell's camp. There were several distinguished officers who also volunteered including Captain James McCall, of Georgia, and Captain Samuel Hammond, of near Ninety-Six. Accounts differ as to the actual number of men, ranging between two hundred and seven hundred. However, it can be assumed that it was sufficient in that there were two enemy camps in the vicinity.

A night ride was chosen since the mission would be successful only if there was swift movement with great secrecy and caution. An hour before sundown on the seventeenth of August, Shelby led the command out of camp with several men acting as guide scouts who were familiar with the countryside. They traveled through dense woods until dark, then moved along a narrow road at a canter that lasted most of the night, without making a single stop. They crossed Gilkey's and Thicketty Creeks, the Pacolet, Fair Forest, Tyger and many other small streams, covering about forty miles on horseback. At daybreak (on the eighteenth) the party halted at the top of a ridge near an old Indian field, one mile from its objective, Musgrove's Ford (Cedar Shoal Creek).

Shelby sent several reliable scouts to reconnoiter who ran into a small party of Tory scouts who had crossed over Musgrove's Ford, and gained their rear. A sharp engagement took place with rapid firing in a wooded area, resulting in one of the enemy being killed and two wounded. Two of

18   **Chapter Three**

the Americans were slightly wounded but were able to return to their comrades and provide intelligence.

They discovered the enemy's army was much larger than first thought. There were several officers present who proved to be highly experienced. In addition they learned from a countryman living nearby that the enemy had been reinforced the evening before with the arrival of Colonel Alexander Innes, from Fort Ninety-Six, with more than six hundred men from the Provincial command known as the "Queen's American Regiment from New York."

"What should we do?" the Patriots asked Shelby. He knew at this point that to give battle to such superior numbers would be fatal to their cause. Also, to retreat with wearied and broken-down horses appeared impossible. Furthermore, it wasn't lost on Shelby that should Ferguson learn of the Americans' presence so close to his camp, he most certainly would jump at the opportunity to fall upon their rear, placing his men in danger of being cut off and captured.

Colonel Shelby and his associates knew that "Death was before them and destruction was behind them." Nevertheless, the decision was made to fight. It was their only true alternative. To procrastinate, or remain inactive for hours, was not wise. It was necessary to bring on an engagement at once, so a strategy of an advance by Captain Shadrack Inman, of Georgia, was approved.

The horses were secured about three hundred yards in the rear in charge of sixteen men. The ground to fight on was selected on a timbered ridge, a short distance from Cedar Shoal Creek, and one-half mile from Musgrove's Mill and ford. The battleline was formed across the road in a semicircle. The men hurried to build a defense out of felled trees, old logs, and brush that they dragged together in thirty minutes. This provided good protection that was about chest high. Shelby occupied the right, Clarke on the left, and Williams in the center. A party of about twenty horsemen was placed on each flank, and within calling distance, there was a reserve of forty men. The stage was set.

The enemy had reached but not crossed the south side of the Enoree River as the Patriots swiftly completed their work. At his own suggestion Captain Inman was sent forward with about twenty-five mounted men to fire upon the enemy and provoke him into crossing the ford. Then, he would retire, keeping up a show of fight so as to draw them into the trap set up for them by the Americans. The ruse was successful. The enemy crossed the river and seemed greatly elated over Inman's retreating before them at the point of their shiny bayonets.

Great shouts of "Huzzah for King George!" filled the air and the sounds of drums and bugle horns could be heard as the advance picked up speed. Within two hundred yards of the American trap they rapidly formed their lines and advanced in a manner as if to anticipate a sudden and complete victory. Moving forward fifty yards they opened fire, but all

Second Cedar Springs and Musgrove's Mill 19

of their musket balls sailed high over the heads of the Patriots who were patiently waiting. Inman continued to carry off his "retreat" with great believability, his movement perfectly describing confusion and chaos within his ranks. Still the enemy pressed on, now getting a bit disorganized and overanxious to settle the matter. Again, they issued another "Huzzah for King George!"

The Americans availed themselves of large tree trunks. Some used the newly constructed barrier for protection and others knelt behind a wooden fence extending along the length of the road. Shelby and Clarke passed the order to hold all fire until the buttons on the enemy's coat could be seen, and then to wait for orders to fire. Each man was "to take his object sure!"

Shelby and Clarke placed their men in one scattered or open line and ordered each to take careful aim. The enemy advanced in three columns, deployed, and fired at the Patriots which was not returned by the center, but by the militia on the right and left. The British next advanced with trailed arms, their columns neatly on display and allowed to come within forty yards when the order "fire" was given. At first fire the enemy ranks recoiled, but the superiority of their numbers and the composure of their officers overcame the moment. Amazingly they managed to reform, rally, and begin a second assault. The struggle turned into a desperate fight, sometimes hand to hand and with the clashing of bayonet against musket barrel. Superior numbers now controlled the outcome. Shelby was finally driven from his line at bayonet point and forced to give up the struggle against uneven numbers. The moment wasn't made any better when he received word that his right flank was beginning to collapse. Clarke struggled to hold his position and managed to send a few reserves that arrived in a timely fashion to stabilize the flank. Then, a break came for the Americans. As Innes was gradually pushing Shelby and Clarke back he fell from his horse, shot by one of the Watauga men, William Smith, who boasted "I have killed their commander!" Innes was carried off to the rear. Receiving word of the fallen leader, Shelby rallied his men and with a regular frontier Indian yell they sprang forward, fighting with great energy, and changed the tide of the battle. As several Tory officers fell, their men began to lose heart and in a short time began their second retreat across the river. The countryside reverberated with the screams and cries of the defeated Tories and British. Together with the moans and cries of the wounded and dying, the sounds from the small battlefield were enormous and greatly frightening. The smoke and din of the battle rose high above the shattered and trampled countryside, and the retreat turned into a complete rout. Shelby's men raced to the river with the wildest fury, loading and firing as they ran. Sword and rifle were used with great authority as they killed, wounded, or captured everyone that came their way. Many Tories threw down their arms and surrendered. Clarke, observing Shelby's success, pressed his men forward.

Chapter Three

One account of the fight noted that "The yells and screeches of the retreating British and Tories as they ran through the woods and over the hills to the river, loudly intermingles with the shouts of their pursuers, together with the groans of the dying and some wounded were terrific and disheartening to the extreme."

The British and Tories carried the greater number into this struggle but in the end were completely routed and did not stop running until completely across the river and into the woods. The battle furious, conducted with small arms alone. The smoke was so dense that a man could not be seen at twenty yards' distance. Colonel Shelby considered it "The hardest and best fought battle he was ever in." He attributed victory to the great valor and persistence of the number of officers who were with him.

The losses of the Loyalists were sixty-three killed, about ninety wounded, and seventy prisoners. Most prominent among their officers who were wounded was Major Fraser. The wound was inflicted by another Watauga man, Robert Beene.

The American losses were only four killed and eight or nine wounded. Few in numbers, but very serious due to the fall of the courageous Captain Inman. He was killed near the junction of the old and new roads between the battle ridge and Musgrove's Ford, while pressing the enemy in a hand-to-hand fight. He received several shots from the Tories with one piercing his forehead.

One of Shelby's best and boldest scouts, Sam Moore, led a small party of ten to twelve upriver and crossed at Head's Ford. From this place he rushed down with such ferocity and audacity as to impress on the enemy that the whole of the army was on them. The enemy immediately increased its speed leaving the scene as Moore and his men retraced their steps and joined their victorious comrades.

One other sidebar to the battle was reported. While the fighting was in progress, many of the British remaining in camp climbed on top of Musgrove's house to witness the result. They never doubted for a moment the success of the troops of King George III. That they would sweep everything before them like an avalanche. When they saw Captain Inman deliver his several volleys of fire near the river and retreat, they threw their hats into the air while they gave out with a resounding huzzah that echoed off the surrounding hills. The opinion of all was that Inman's small force was all the Americans had at hand and it was reasonable to think that the fight was over before it really started. When they saw their men driven backwards and routed by the Whig forces their faces were covered with disbelief and consternation. Fearing capture by the Americans and long before they had crossed the river, they had repacked their knapsacks and were on the road to Ninety-Six. It was said that about fifty of this number were paroled prisoners doing duty contrary to law.

Second Cedar Springs and Musgrove's Mill 21

A large, British patrolling party that had arrived at Jones' Ford, down river, heard the gunfire and galloped at full speed to the scene. They were briefed by an officer and then dashed boldly across the river but were too late. The Americans were gone. Unknown to Shelby at the time was that the British received reinforcements soon after the battle from Fort Ninety-Six.

Shelby and Clarke seriously considered following up their success by making a dash for Fort Ninety-Six in southwestern South Carolina. The fort was given the name of this one-time Indian gathering place, by the Indians, because it was ninety-six miles from a principal village farther south and ninety-six miles to another large village to the north. It was converted into a fort by the Tories, aided by the Indians.

The strategy changed when an express messenger, named Francis Jones, arrived in great haste from McDowell's headquarters with a letter written by North Carolina Governor Richard Caswell, telling of the tremendous loss of General Horatio Gates' Patriot army near Camden, South Carolina on the sixteenth. Apparently, Caswell had been there. His letter advised McDowell and all of his officers to get out of the way at once as they were in danger of being cut off. McDowell sent word that he would move at once to Gilbert Town. Shelby, familiar with the governor's handwriting, recognized the letter as not being a Tory trick. The advance to Ninety-Six was abandoned.

Shelby saw at once the danger he and his associates were in. They could not retire to McDowell's camp at Smith's Ford, for he was no longer there. Gates' army, except for those who were either killed or captured, was widely scattered. Ferguson was on his flank and there were British at Ninety-Six. The only option was to march to the northwest and elude Ferguson.

This dictated a retreat to the mountains for safety to elude Ferguson who must know of the fight and be on his way to release the prisoners. Shelby led the line in a northwesterly direction, accompanied by their prisoners, who were distributed three to each American and required to carry a gun deprived of the flint.

He ordered a non-stop effort that lasted both day and night, for two days, stopping only long enough to take a drink of fresh water from a creek and to pull peaches or green corn from along the roadside, which was consumed raw. (Accounts of the exact route vary greatly.)

Late in the evening of the eighteenth, Ferguson's party reached a spot where the Whigs had, less than thirty minutes before, fed their weary horses, but not knowing how long the Americans had been gone, and finding his men and horses exhausted, the pursuit was abandoned. Not aware of this, the Americans kept on their steady route and the next day, passing the North Tyger, entered North Carolina. This was sixty miles from the battlefield and one hundred miles from Smith's Ford (via Musgrove's Mill) from where they had started without making a stop except to fight, all

Chapter Three

the while loaded down with seventy, sometimes obnoxious, prisoners. The rapid march took its toll on the Patriots. They arrived at McDowell's camp near Gilbert Town in central North Carolina with their faces swollen and eyes bloated from hunger and fatigue. Shelby transferred the prisoners to Colonel Clarke and then to Colonel Williams for delivery to Hillsboro.

Colonel Shelby proposed that an army be raised at once from both sides of the mountains in numbers sufficient to cope with Ferguson. Officers and privates were both consulted and all agreed to the proposal and the feasibility of its undertaking. It was agreed that the over-the-mountain men would return at once to their homes to recruit and strengthen their numbers, as the term of their present service had expired. Colonel McDowell, in the meantime, was to remain in front of Ferguson to obtain information on his movements and to keep the over-the-mountain men informed. He sent an express to Colonels Benjamin Cleveland and Herndon, of Wilkes County, and Major Joseph Winston, of Surry County, inviting them to join in the expedition soon to be organized against Ferguson.

McDowell also went about devising ways to keep the beef stock of the Whigs in the Upper Catawba Valley hidden from Ferguson. He knew this would soon be one of the objectives. Shelby and Clarke, after a brief reunion with McDowell, parted company. Shelby and Major James Robinson, with their Holstein and Watauga volunteers, took the trail that led to their homes over the Alleghenies. Colonel Clark returned to Georgia via the mountain trails.

It has been recorded that after the Battle of Musgrove's that for many miles around every woman and child who was able to leave their home visited the battlefield. It was chiefly a Tory region and most of the visitors were Loyalists. Bodies of the dead were turned over to see if they could identify a missing father or brother. Some went away with saddened hearts. Some removed remains from the field to bury elsewhere. The nearby Musgrove's farm and mill were turned into a hospital. A few of the Americans who were wounded were left behind when the Tories finally departed. They were cared for by the Allan Musgrove family, whose ancestors emigrated from England.

Colonel Inman was buried near the farm under a Spanish oak where he fell. A marker identifies the location today. Another grave contained the bodies of sixteen Tories.

Chapter Four

☆☆☆☆☆☆☆☆☆☆☆☆☆☆☆
Going after Ferguson

After Musgrove's, a period of darkness descended on the Carolinas. In the wake of the enormous British victories at Charleston and Camden, many citizens, reasoning that the war was lost, went into the British and Tory camps to align themselves with the crown. Wanting to be on the winning side, it appeared that the Patriot cause had been lost for good. There was no organized American army anywhere in the Carolinas. The Crown's flag floated in the cool breezes over Charleston and Savannah as General Cornwallis laid plans to inflict further strife and carnage on the opposition. He wrote to Colonel John Harris Cruger at Fort Ninety-Six the following:

"I have given orders that all of the inhabitants of this providence, who are not submitted and who had taken part in the revolt, should be punished with the greatest rigor; that they should be imprisoned and their whole property taken from them and destroyed. I have likewise directed that compensation should be made out of their effort to the persons who have been plundered and oppressed by them. I have ordered in the most positive manner, that *every militia man who had borne arms with us and afterwards joined the enemy, should be immediately hanged*! I have now, sir, only to desire that you will take the most vigorous measures to *extinguish the rebellion* in the district in which you command, and that you will obey in the strictest manner, the directions I have given in this letter, relative to the treatment of the country." (Italics added by author.)

Thereafter followed a purge of the countryside by Cornwallis' senior officers that wrote an even darker chapter to the war's history. In those days it was no small matter to oppose or confront the authority of Great Britain, the mightiest monarchy on earth. The Americans were mere upstarts that must be taught a severe lesson in obedience. No doubt, Cornwallis would have scoffed at an old saying that would eventually prove to be true that "it is sometimes darkest before the dawn!"

24   **Chapter Four**

Shelby and the other Patriot leaders had gone to their homes as the terms of their volunteers' enlistment had expired. The Patriots returned to the vastness of the mountains, the Old Spartan district, the Holston Valley, the Watauga, and the Catawba. With the Americans disbursed, Ferguson became undisputed master of the country. He marched through several districts, plundering as he went, destroying the citizens' cattle, homes, horses, beds, clothing, and even jerking rings from the fingers of the women.

The British, being unable to control General George Washington's army in the north, decided in 1779 to shift the war to the southern states. Along the way British warships bombarded and raided many coastal towns. As told before, Charleston was subdued and the only Patriot army in the south was eliminated by the forces of King George. At this time General Cornwallis hit upon a plan to bring the war to an end. The Crown was being stretched to the extreme as France and Spain entered the conflict on the American side and Parliament was exerting pressure on its military leaders to bring the war in America to a successful close as soon as possible. After all, it was costing huge amounts of money to finance a "world war."

Cornwallis plotted to divide the colonies (actually states, since by act of Congress in September 1776, the name of America was hereafter to be known as the "United States of America," instead of "United Colonies of America"). The plan was simple. He would send columns of men northward on three major routes. One would move near the coastline to guarantee continued uninterrupted supplies from the navy. A second would sweep through the middle of the Carolinas into Virginia, Maryland, and Pennsylvania, then turn eastward through the Northern towns and cities to the coast. The move would split the country and end the conflict in England's favor.

The third column would march to the west into the mountain sections of the two Carolinas and would deliver a finishing blow to the "backwater men" as they were known. These men had been "harassing" Tory outposts and disrupting the king's work. It was decided that professional soldiers dispose of these pests who run and hide after their sneak attacks.

Named to head this western thrust was one of the most capable soldiers serving in the British army in America, Major Patrick Ferguson. A scholar, born to wealth, he was an inventor, master horseman, and had a flair for fighting. Ferguson set about his assignment with 1,500 troops. All were Americans, trained and armed by the British. Ferguson would be the only true Brit in the small army. He made his way quickly to Gilbert Town where he had heard the Americans were in camp. Not finding them there he developed a plan to intimidate the men from over the mountain. He released a Patriot prisoner named Samuel Phillips, a relative of Shelby, with the following message. "That if they did not desist from their opposition to

Going after Ferguson 25

British arms, he (Ferguson) would march his army over the mountains, hang their leaders and lay their country waste by fire and sword. Signed Major Patrick Ferguson, 71st Regiment."

Phillips went directly to Shelby with the message, but instead of intimidating him, Ferguson's message had the opposite reaction. With determination, Shelby proposed an army of men from both sides of the mountains be brought together to deal with Ferguson. Most of the officers and men at this time agreed with the idea. To augment his proposed army, Shelby rode some forty miles on horseback to present-day Jonesboro, Tennessee to see his friend Colonel John Sevier and others.

He alerted Sevier, a tough, old Indian fighter, to Ferguson's intention and together the two leaders determined that the effort outlined by Shelby would be worth the try if they could enlist the services of Colonel William Campbell, of Washington County, Virginia. Campbell was a frequent hunting companion of Daniel Boone. He commanded several hundred Patriots who would do themselves proud in the coming battle. If so, the two would raise the men needed for the expedition against the hated Ferguson and his Loyalists.

Shelby wrote later that "If Campbell hesitated, or even refused, then we would turn and cooperate with any corps of the Army of the United States with which we might meet. If all failed and the country was overrun with British red, we determined to take to the waters of the streams and rivers and go down to the Spaniards in Louisiana."A messenger was sent speeding to Campbell's home in lower Virginia and while the two warriors awaited his reply, both set about gathering men and arms.

Meanwhile, Ferguson continued his acts of intimidation. Another note was written and this time it was posted by couriers at every crossroads and country store in the "backwater" area. It read,

> To the inhabitants of North Carolina, Gentlemen. Unless you wish to be eat up by an inundation of barbarians who have begun by murdering an unarmed son before the eyes of his aged father [a falsehood meant to inflame opinion] I say if you wish to be pinioned, robbed and murdered and see your wives and daughters abused by these dregs of mankind, grasp your arms and come to our camp. The backwater men have crossed the mountains. If you choose to be set upon by mongrels, say so at once and let your men turn their backs on you and look for real men to protect you. Patrick Ferguson, 71st Regiment.

These notes caused an uprising among the mountain people who looked upon their land as their own and their homes as places of safety for their families. Only infrequent Indian raids spoiled the quiet, hard work, making a living out of the land.

When Shelby returned to his home he was greeted with demands that something be done about this hothead Ferguson. He explained that his absence had been to enlist the services of Sevier and Campbell. Sevier

26   **Chapter Four**

was in their camp but he had not heard from Campbell whose home was to the north. Messengers were dispatched by Shelby across the countryside and to both sides of the mountains, asking for a gathering of mountain men to launch a hunt for Ferguson and face him in battle. Shelby spoke for his countrymen when he said, "It is better that we go after him, than he come after us!"

The messengers carried the word of the planned attack against Ferguson and of a gathering of backwater men. The date was set for September 25, 1780, at Sycamore Shoals on the Watauga River, in northwestern North Carolina.

Shelby was greatly pleased with the responses to his appeal for assistance. A week before the gathering he had assembled more than two hundred men, all backwoodsmen, all proven Indian fighters familiar with the ways of the woods in combat.

The trip to the shoals was a short one for the men from Sullivan County. Shelby was the first to arrive on the twenty-fourth. During the early morning hours small groups of men in coonskin caps arrived, some on foot others mounted. At noon the sound of cheers were heard as Colonel Campbell arrived with two hundred armed men and announced that another two hundred would be in camp before the day was out.

Making the trip with Colonel Shelby were his two brothers, Major Evan Shelby Jr. (the third) and Captain Moses Shelby.

The next day spirits rose even higher with the arrival of Sevier and his contingent that numbered several hundred. Riding alongside this stately hero of the backwoods were his two sons: Joseph, 18, and James, 16, along with two brothers, Valentine and Robert.

John Crockett, father of the legendary frontier fighter Davy Crockett, rode into the camp of his friend Campbell. There were three other Crocketts present—Joseph, Walter, and William. And an amazing twelve Campbells, all related to the colonel. The small army also boasted fifty-nine men with "Mc" in their names. A good illustration of the Scotch-Irish presence.

Shelby and Sevier took it upon themselves to find powder and food for the gathering fighters, which came from an unexpected place. John Adair was the entryman for Sullivan County. His latest collections amounted to $12,735 from land sales. However, due to a crisis with marauding Indians he had been unable to deliver the funds to the state treasury. He said to Shelby, "It belongs to North Carolina, but if the country is overrun by the British, then Liberty is lost. So let the money go too. Take it." And with that, Adair and his son signed on with the army. Adair was 78 years old.

Sevier and Shelby assured Adair that the debt would be repaid in full, which it wasn't. Two years later, the North Carolina legislature approved the actions of the mountain men and forgave the debt in full.

Monday, September 25, dawned bright and clear at Sycamore Shoals. (Site today of Elizabethtown, Tennessee.) This was where Judge Richard

Going after Ferguson   27

Henderson had bargained with the many Indian chiefs to negotiate the sale of Kain-Tuck. Today, Hendersonville, Kentucky carries his name.

As the hours passed more men arrived to swell the army's numbers. By late evening more than 1,000 had gathered. Many were sons accompanying their fathers along with women and daughters.

The dress among these uncommon backwater men was common. No one wore a military uniform. A hunting shirt, girded with beads, and trousers, made from homespun with leggings, and a coonskin cap, stuck with bucktails, was their usual dress. At the belt line there hung a long scalping knife, a tomahawk, a short bag of parched corn, and a tin cup. A powder horn was slung around the neck to fuel his deadly Dickert rifle, often referred to as the Kentucky rifle. The rifle was invented by John Dickert of Lancaster, Pennsylvania. It had a barrel 30 inches long with a spiral groove that gave it amazing accuracy at long distance. Each man was an expert with his knife and rifle, having honed his skills in many fights with wild game and the marauding Indians.

As the time for marching drew near the Reverend Samuel Doak, a black-frocked Presbyterian minister, stood before them on a tree stump to deliver a message and blessing. Opening his long arms toward the heavens, he quoted from the Holy Bible, Judges 6:7. It told the story of how Gideon and an elite corps of men with no previous military experience drove out the great hordes of Midianites who had infested the land of Israel like locust. He described how God blessed Gideon and an angel instructed his 300 carefully selected men. Into the enemy camp they rushed with the sound of trumpets blasting, shouting as they went, "The sword of the Lord and Gideon!" Divinely inspired they slew the enemy in great numbers and drove him from their land. And there was great jubilation in victory and glorifying the Lord.

At the end of this greatly inspiring sermon the mountain men leaped to their feet, shook their rifles over their heads, and in one great voice repeatedly shouted, "The sword of the Lord and Gideon! The sword of the Lord and Gideon!" And like slow, cascading thunder the reply echoed off the hillsides. "The sword of the Lord and Gideon!" Each man felt divinely inspired at the moment and felt within himself that the hated Ferguson would be vanquished.

The excitement and anticipation of the coming fight permeated the camp that night. It was after midnight before quiet settled over the small army, and some could be heard making up songs that contained their new battle cry, "The sword of the Lord and Gideon." Many wives and relatives remained to cook hearty meals for the men the next morning and to pack supplies for the long march ahead.

Shelby was up before dawn, organizing the line of march that would include several hundred head of cattle for food. After breakfast and final good-byes to families and friends, the journey began. Some still liked to

28   Chapter Four

remind the others of the battle cry inspired by Pastor Doak's sermon. It could be heard spoken and sung as the marchers fell into line behind their leaders. Shelby pointed the line south to an area between Greer and Jenkins Mountains, then eastward around the shoulder of Stone Mountain and Ripshin Ridge on the Doe River. The first day's march covered twenty miles and spirits remained high.

The following morning the march resumed and at midday reached the foot of Roan Mountain. At this point Shelby realized that he would be unable to take the herd of cattle across the steep incline and dangerous paths. He ordered that the herd be slaughtered and a feast be prepared. By mid-afternoon, with their bellies full, the march continued on the road to Carver's Gap, whose summit extends 5,512 feet above sea level. At the end of the second day's march Shelby's men struggled to the 3,832-foot level where the air was thin and the snow was ankle deep. At this point Shelby and Sevier conducted a full "dress" parade only to discover that two of their number were missing. Shelby assumed that the two were on their way to inform Ferguson, who would probably come to meet them accompanied by the feared Cherokee Indians. A decision was made to change their route to avoid a possible ambush. Some of the men suggested turning back since their plan would be in British hands very soon and that they had now lost the element of surprise. Many had not dressed for the higher altitudes and snow, but had not complained until now. However, the majority insisted that they continue on. Colonel McDowell selected a handful of men and went on ahead to scout and to obtain information of Ferguson's whereabouts.

On the third day the line of march was toward the eastern crest of the Blue Ridge with the profile of Grandfather Mountain on their left. The army was divided into two. One-half went north and the others went east to North Cove where McDowell rejoined them with the news that Ferguson was at Gilbert Town, and idle. Shelby immediately felt better about the mission. The chances of catching Ferguson off guard were brighter, and the news also cheered the men.

The following day Linville Mountain was crossed and the road turned south to the head of Paffy Creek where Campbell and the other half of the army appeared. Spirits remained high and the talk of "getting Ferguson" continued, as the army, now at full strength, advanced. Next, the march continued to the broad Quaker Meadows, 4,500 feet below the Bald of Roan and into warmer weather. A celebration was ordered for their five-day victory over the mountains and cold weather conditions and another feast was held. This time they fed on cattle that valley farmers had hidden from the British when they came looking for food only a few days before.

Shelby and Sevier were elated to learn that Colonel Benjamin Cleveland, of Burke County, would soon join their ranks with 350 men. And that Major Joseph Winston was due soon with 200 fighters from Surry

Going after Ferguson

County. (Winston would later lend his name to the first half of a new village in North Carolina, Winston-Salem. The sword presented to him after King's Mountain can be seen today in the old Salem Museum.) Both were veterans of many Indian fights and each wore the wounds as proof.

On October 1 the army had increased in size to 1,500 men. Confidence remained extremely high. After marching from Quaker Meadows, the army was within one day's march of Gilbert Town and Ferguson's troops who had been trained by the British. Major Ferguson was the only British soldier present.

As the time for battle neared Colonel Campbell was selected to overall command and Major McDowell would command the men from Burke County.

Shelby came before the army with the following general order. "When we reach the enemy don't wait for the word of command, let each of you be your own officer and do the best you can. If in the woods, shelter yourselves and give them Indian play. The moment the enemy gives way, be on the alert and strictly obey orders."

Again the battle cry went up as the backwater men anticipated the coming confrontation with Ferguson. He would be the number one target of every rifleman once the engagement commenced.

As the army set forth moving to Gilbert Town the next morning, the officers learned from a Patriot that Ferguson had sent to Lord Cornwallis for help, advising him of the advancing backwater men and that he would find himself a nice elevated hill from where he would wait. He would defy the Almighty and all the Rebels out of hell to drive him off. Ferguson said he was tired of running after a bunch of banditti. Unfortunately for Ferguson, the messenger was captured by Patriots. A second note to the commander at Fort Ninety-Six was also intercepted.

Shelby and the other officers agreed that if Ferguson was to be taken it would have to be soon, within the next two days if possible. Meanwhile, cheers went up from the riflemen as they welcomed fifty more men into their ranks. All were from the south fork of the Catawba under Major William Chronicle, and all were mounted on fresh horses.

As time for action drew close the officers streamlined the army for rapid movement. All sick men and those without mounts were left behind along with the foot soldiers of Major Joseph Herndon of Wilkes County. Wilkes made notes in his records of the event that the attack army numbered seven hundred.

Ferguson always considered the mountain men a pack of mongrels from which he could run or turn and fight, winning an easy victory. They were not organized and did not understand the methods of modern warfare. He had no intention of turning tail and running to Charlotte for protection. His men were well trained and would fight well for the Crown, regardless of how many banditti confronted him.

30   **Chapter Four**

On October 5, Ferguson wrote again to Lord Cornwallis. "The opposition has, I understand, become somewhat of a consequence. I am on the march on a road leading from Cherokee Ford, north of King's Mountain. Three or four hundred good soldiers, part dragoons should finish this business. Something must be done. This is their last push in this quarter and they are extremely desolate."

Ironically, the two officers who could have gone to Ferguson's aid at this time were Tarleton, who was sick with malaria, and Cornwallis, who had taken to his bed with a bad cold. Why none of their subordinates acted on information they eventually received is not known.

Chapter Five

☆☆☆☆☆☆☆☆☆☆☆☆☆☆☆
The Score Is Settled

On Friday, October 6, amid great fanfare and high spirits Ferguson marched out of his camp at 4 a.m. The weather was fair, the Union Jack snapped in the breeze, and his men joked about the "over-mountain men" that they might later battle. Many of them they knew personally.

After a trouble-free sixteen miles the British officer selected a defensive position on Little King's Mountain.

Again he wrote Cornwallis. "I have arrived today at King's Mountain and have taken a post where I do not think I can be forced by a stronger enemy than that against me. I am on a march toward you by a road leading from Cherokee Ford, north of King's Mountain. Two or three-hundred good soldiers, part dragoons, would finish this business. Something must be done soon. This is their last push in this quarter...I am the king of the mountain."

At this time Ferguson had with him one hundred troops drawn from the King William American Regiment, the Queen's Rangers, and the New Jersey Volunteers, along with about one thousand Loyalist militia. His message to his commanding officer paints a picture of utter contempt for his enemy. Yet, he admits to his strength and knowing this offers no hint that he would march to join the army's main body, which he could have easily done.

On the same day the Patriot army entered South Carolina it arrived at Cowpens, named for the gigantic herds of cattle that could be found there throughout the year. It was owned by a Tory named Hiram Sanders, and in the near future would be the scene of a great battle waged by the Patriots. The question on everyone's mind at this time remained the same, "Where is Ferguson?"

The question of Ferguson's whereabouts was answered in an unexpected way. Joseph Kerr, a cripple from infancy and a master spy, appeared before Shelby and Sevier with valuable intelligence only six hours old. Kerr, pointing dramatically to the northeast, said that Ferguson had

32   **Chapter Five**

stopped at noon to eat at a plantation only six miles from King's Mountain and his troop strength was estimated at fifteen hundred. The Patriot officers accepted the intelligence with jubilant gratitude and immediately gave orders to break camp. Scouts were hurried off to pinpoint the enemy's exact position as soon as possible. Along the way they learned that a band of Tories, on their way to join Ferguson, had learned of the advancing backwater men, and had disbursed and gone home.

At 8 p.m. Shelby started his mounted columns from Cowpens to the east on a course to the Broad River and King's Mountain. The sky was moonless and rain began to fall.

In the darkness some of the guides, leading Campbell's men, became confused and lost their way. Colonel William Hill wrote that the paths for marching were very narrow and the woods so thick that many of his men spent the night wandering about. Shelby, when learning of the mishap, scattered a number of scouts in all directions to locate the missing corps which was located and put on the correct path again to rejoin the main body. The columns marched at a furious pace causing many of their horses to give out since most had not been shod. Despite the fatigue the pace was maintained. The goal was too near to make camp and rest.

In the morning the lead column arrived at Cherokee Ford, on the Broad River. Another group of scouts was ordered to determine if Ferguson may have set a trap. One of the scouts was Enoc Gilmer, a multitalented, fearless individual who could have the men laughing one minute and then the next, convinced that he was a raving maniac, completely insane. He was gone for several hours and on his return through the damp woods he could be heard singing a favorite song of the Virginians, "Barney-Lynn," giving the signal that all was safe for the time being.

As the time for action was imminent, the army waded the cold waters while the officers ordered all guns wrapped in blankets to keep them dry. This order brought muffled laughter from the jaded mountain men who thought it was most obvious. Some of the men who had been in the saddle for almost 24 consecutive hours began to grumble, saying they were hungry. The officers relented and gave permission for the stripping clean of a nearby cornfield. One soldier had brought with him a cow bar, or utter, and cooked it to go with his corn. The march continued for another mile when a scout galloped toward Shelby saying Ferguson was six miles ahead and motionless.

At this moment, as if by an omen, the sun came out, a cool breeze began to blow, and the men stopped their grumbling. Scouts continued to aggressively inquire of local citizens about Ferguson's whereabouts. At one roadside house several of Sevier's men talked with a farmer without any luck. He did not know of Ferguson or where he might be. He was thanked and as the scouts walked through the front door onto a small porch, they were followed by a tiny girl. In defiance of her father she ran into the road where two mounted scouts were about to leave, and asked

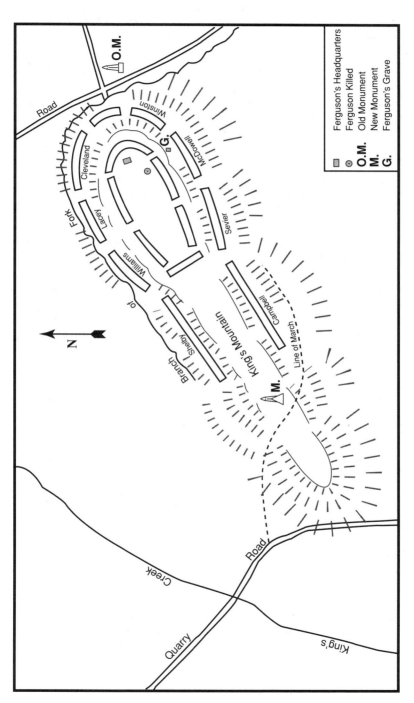

Map of the Battle of King's Mountain

King's Mountain

34   **Chapter Five**

with great animation and in a loud, high-pitched voice, "How many of there are you?"

"Enough to whip Ferguson when we catch up with him," a scout answered, smiling at his young inquisitor.

Casting a quick eye toward the front porch of her home where her father was motioning her to keep quiet, she wheeled about and pointed to a range about three miles distant and exclaimed, "He is on THAT mountain!" Immediately she ran into the house avoiding the punishing eyes of her father.

On hearing the news the officers' faces brightened, understanding that their long, laborious journey was to climax and the long time spent away from their wives and families would soon be over.

The Patriots rode swiftly down the road to alert the others. Someone noticed Enoc Gilmer's horse tied up in front of a Tory house. The officers leading the column raced to the house and dismounted in the front yard. Inside the small house they found Gilmer at the table, eating a feast and being attended by two women. William Campbell produced a rope with a noose and shouted at the top of his voice, "You damned rascal, at last we have caught up with you!" Gilmer carried off his role in true thespian tradition pleading for mercy as Campbell placed the rope around his neck. Campbell bellowed that he would hang Gilmer from the nearest tree as he dragged him out of the house into the front yard. As Gilmer was dragged, kicking and screaming to several nearby trees, the rope was thrown over a low branch with Gilmer still pleading. Suddenly the two women began to cry and moan loudly from the front porch of their home when William Chronicle intervened. Gilmer was then put on a horse, declared a prisoner, and rode away still begging for his life. When out of sight of the women Gilmer told his story. He had arrived at the house and identified himself as a friend of the king, who wished to locate and join up with Ferguson. The two women admitted that they too were friends of the king and each planted a big kiss on Gilmer's cheek. One admitted that only a few hours before she had taken some chickens to Ferguson's camp on a ridge between two streams on a spur of King's Mountain.

At this point and with twice confirmed intelligence, Shelby, the real leader of the mountain men, called a war council. It would be a simple matter, he reasoned, to surround Ferguson if they had enough men. The idea was immediately approved and as the mountain men would be shooting uphill there would be little danger of them hitting each other. This would be a contest of Whig against Tory, not American against the British, and the numbers would be about equal. The Tory would have his bayonet and the Patriots, or Whigs, with their long rifles were suited perfectly for this kind of fighting.

Ferguson's men were well trained and were led by competent officers. As the Patriot officers continued to develop their plan, a lone rider

The Score Is Settled   35

who galloped at full speed off the hill and into the arms of several of the mountain men was brought before Shelby and Williams. He was another messenger from Ferguson to Cornwallis, this time asking for help! The young horseman, in the grasp of several muscular Patriots, exhibited great fright and in a shaking voice divulged all. He said that Ferguson was on the hill and he was wearing a checkered shirt in the manner of a duster over his uniform. Because of an earlier war wound to his right hand he would command with his sword in his left hand.

As the word spread the men bellowed a controlled cheer and prepared for battle with the hated Ferguson and his Tory soldiers. The plan of attack was as Shelby suggested. The mountain, where Ferguson had positioned his men behind slaty ledges around the summit, would be surrounded at its base by the mountain men. When the order to advance was given, the ring would be closed as the Americans moved upwards, constantly decreasing the diameter of the circle until the mountain had been scaled and Ferguson eliminated!

King's Mountain stretches from North Carolina into South Carolina for about sixteen miles, describing an angle extending from the northeast to the southwest that was not very high. Ferguson chose to defend an area six miles southwest of a peak known as "The Principle." The range takes its name from a man named King who lived at its foot many years ago. Ferguson, not knowing its history, considered it a good symbol and swore that he would hold it for his king (George III). The site is two miles inside South Carolina and rises only sixty feet above the level plains. Its ridge is about 600 yards long and very narrow from base to base. Its heavily wooded slopes were steep, and its long, oval top had been cleared of trees. It measured about 400 yards in length and was twenty to forty yards wide.

The Patriot command was divided into four parts and would be lead four abreast to a point from which the separate columns would move to their respective positions. The interior lines would be composed of men from Virginia and Sullivan Counties. Campbell would lead his men in the right column and Shelby on the left. The right flank column would consist of men from Surry, Nolachucky, and Burke Counties directed by Major Winston. The detachment under Major McDowell was joined to Sevier.

The left flank column was composed of men from Wilkes County and those who joined the previous days from the two Carolinas under Colonel Williams. In all, the two columns amounted to about two regiments. The intentions of this small army was to not only attack and defeat the enemy on the hill but to bring about its annihilation.

At three o'clock the leaders put the columns in motion toward the bottom of the ravine north of the mountain. Then, the two interior columns halted, dismounted, tied their mounts to trees, and left a small group of men in charge. The left column continued forward.

Shelby's men were deployed near the roadway to attack the eastern extremity of the ridge. Sevier and Campbell were on his right. These men

36   Chapter Five

were the first to take position and had the most difficult terrain to traverse due to the sharpness of the slope and the height of the crest. In rapid succession the other units moved quickly to their assigned positions, dismounted, and prepared for the fight.

The commanders cautioned their men to hold their fire until near the enemy and to reform ranks if broken and renew the fight. Shelby told his men to "see what you shoot and shoot what you see!" Then the order was passed to "Prime your guns!"

The countersign for the battle would be "Buford."

This was in honor of Colonel Abraham Buford, who with a force of 350 Virginia Continentals and cavalry had retreated from Cornwallis after his victory at Charleston. The British commander sent 270 green-coated dragoons after Buford under Lt. Col. Sir Banastre Tarleton. Tarleton, who was short and stalky, with red hair, was a British officer without battlefield morals. Vanquish was his byword, and do it as quickly and completely as possible. He was 26 years of age and a graduate of Oxford University. A vociferous braggard about the many women he had conquered, he swore, just as loudly, to do the same to the Southern Rebels.

After a fast-paced ride of 54 hours, covering 105 miles, Tarleton caught up with Buford on May 29, 1780, at a place called Waxhaws in a small area just south of the border of the two Carolinas. Buford who was quickly surrounded and overrun by the British-mounted infantry surrendered.

Under Buford's white flag the two officers began negotiating surrender terms. Tarleton greatly exaggerated his troop strength by 500, claiming 700 when he had only 200. He demanded Buford's surrender which was politely refused. Great confusion erupted suddenly between both sides. Tarleton's men, under the allegation that some Americans had fired after the white flag was raised, were allowed to pierce the men who had surrendered with their bayonets, and thereafter they entered into an orgy of ruthless butchery, slaying 113 unarmed Americans as they screamed for quarter, a plea never refused a vanquished foe. Another 203 Patriots were seriously wounded and captured. Half of these were dead in three days, having been hacked to pieces and left without medical attention.

Patriots who came upon this repulsive scene later described the mutilation of the Americans as deliberate. Evidence indicated that the "carving" was done after the brave men had fallen to the ground. Teeth were smashed in and faces slashed by sabers in various patterns. Bodies were carved up as if by a butcher. *This atrocity was unmatched in the entire war* and did not go without notice by the Patriots now assembled at the foot of King's Mountain. Word of the massacre spread like wildfire among the Carolinas and sparked the flame of revenge in the hearts of all Whigs and had a swaying effect on many who were still undecided in the conflict. It also gave birth to the phrase that every Continental soldier would

The Score Is Settled 37

henceforth carry on his lips when engaged with the enemy. "Tarleton's Quarter" carried with it the determination to liberate the United States for good from the hated British beast.

Ferguson's Provincials wore the traditional red coats and white breeches of the regular army. However, few of the more than 1,000 that he had trained wore anything resembling a British uniform. Many had pinned a paper, or cloth cockade, to their hats to distinguish them from their neighbors on the other side.

All of his men were American Loyalists, armed with the old reliable "Brown Bess" musket, complete with bayonet. He had trained his men to jam their bayonets down their rifle barrels when ammunition was spent, or if they were unable to load when charged. His men would have cold steel available when the enemy had only its gun butts as a club.

Ferguson had with him his cook, two mistresses, and two officers in which he had supreme confidence: Captains Abraham dePeyster, of New York, and Alexander Chesney, of South Carolina.

At mid-afternoon several Tory officers made their rounds of the whole northern half of the ridge, checking on their men and found no trace of the enemy in any area. Perhaps their elevated position had, after all, discouraged any foolhardy attack on this fortress. Should one come, however, the Americans would certainly pay a high price. There was great consolation in such thoughts.

Captain Chesney had just completed his afternoon rounds, checking with pickets stationed in the woods at the foot of the hill. All reported no sign of the enemy. The Tory force, except for the guards, rested in their tents until a rain shower passed and then relaxed in the sunlight. Chesney was about to enter Ferguson's tent to make his report when a shot rang out in the woods below the hilltop. He immediately called his men to the direction of the shot, posted his officers, and was about to issue another order when a bullet killed his horse. Falling to the ground with his horse, he was able to avoid being pinned under the huge, dead animal. He stood up to observe where the firing was coming from and to determine how many of the enemy were present. A moment later another bullet wounded him and the battle was on! Ferguson rushed to the officer's side and heard him say, "Things are ominous! Those are the same yelling devils I fought at Musgrove's Mill!"

From the north side of the hill came loud, savage-style war whoops. A few at first and then many. Ferguson leaped from his tent, mounted his white horse, and began furiously shouting orders to his officers. Around his neck was a chain holding a silver whistle. By this means he could convey various orders to his men who were trained to hear its shrill blasts depending on the number blown. As it became evident that the enemy

38   **Chapter Five**

was attacking him from several points he shifted the troops to where they seemed to be needed the most. Gradually the war whoops grew louder, some were close and others were distant beyond the edge of the hill. His men dashed from tree to tree, looking the slopes for targets to fire at and often when they sighted one they would overshoot.

On the order to advance, the backwoodsmen crept up the hill Indian fashion and opened fire from the cover of trees and thick bushes. It is believed that Phillip Greever, of Washington County, Virginia, fired the first shot that day. Greever said after the battle that he "ran up the mountain [and] when I saw a Tory behind a tree, who I shot at, which I believe was the first gun fired."

Ferguson's men fought back and in a few minutes repulsed Campbell's men who had reached the top first, having the shortest distance to climb.

Robert Henry, a sixteen year old, was there: "Enoch Gilmer called on Hugh Erwin, Adam Berry, and myself to follow him close to the foot of the hill. We marched with a quick step, letting Major Chronicle advance about ten steps before us, but further from the hill we were until we met the wing [Winston's] from the other side of the hill. Then, Chronicle having a militant hat, clapped his hand to it in front and raised it up and cried, 'Face the hill!' The words were scarcely uttered when a ball struck him and he dropped; and a second later a ball struck William Rabb, about six feet from Chronicle, and he dropped. We then advanced up the hill close to the Tory line."

Captain William Edmondson led his men forward as the bullets began to fly hotter and faster and ran into a bayonet charge from the hilltop. He fired at one of the Tories, then clubbed him with the butt of his gun, and knocked the enemy's gun out of his hands. Seizing the soldier by the neck, he made him a prisoner, and brought him back to the bottom of the hill. Edmondson quickly returned to his men on the hillside and in directing their actions was mortally wounded. The Tories fired several rounds and then initiated a spirited bayonet charge, driving the Americans back down the hill.

As other Patriots neared the summit they began to pick off Ferguson's men at an accelerated pace. Twice, Ferguson directed bayonet charges and drove the mountain men back, but each time the frontiersmen rallied.

On Campbell's left, Shelby's men were in motion. The hill they were climbing was steep and rocky and required a longer period to negotiate. As they neared the top they were detected by a Tory who sounded the alarm to Ferguson. Before Shelby's men could get in a good position to open fire Ferguson shifted his men again to meet the new challenge.

Halfway up the hill and among Shelby's men there was a wounded Tory named Drury Mathas. He survived the fight and later recorded his observations of the mountain men. He said, "They seemed like devils from the infernal regions and were the most powerful men physically I have ever seen. They were tall, raw-boned and with long, matted hair."

Ferguson directed a rigorous bayonet charge against Shelby's men as they struggled to gain the hilltop. Remembering their orders, they fell back in good order, shooting as they went. Again the shrill sound of Ferguson's whistle brought his men back to the top of the hill to meet a third challenge, this time from Cleveland's men on Shelby's left. The men from Surrey County had problems with the large outcropping of rocks but managed to work their way up, climbing steadily, and stopping to shoot at anything that moved. "Shoot at anything that moves!" Cleveland screamed above the growing din of gunfire. With increased effort his men threw caution to the wind and struggled among the trees and rocks to the top. "Just a little closer," Cleveland urged his charges. "Just a little closer!"

As the circle began to close on Ferguson, Winston's followers ran into some difficulty in finding their assigned position. Their position was very important because it lay across Ferguson's only route of escape, eastward to Charlotte. The guide assigned to lead him there had lost sight of the ridge on which the enemy was positioned. An unidentified officer rode into sight waving his hat in the air to attract Winston's attention. He ordered Winston to dismount his men and march up the hill in front of them. The order was obeyed and off went his command, plunging into heavy brush and climbing over rocky formations. Winston realized in ten minutes that it was the wrong hill, so he returned to the bottom, exhausted and dismayed. In moments the same officer reappeared and this time shouted, "Come quick, the enemy is a mile ahead! Mount your horses and push on!"

The men ran to their horses, mounted, and rode like fox hunters through the undergrowth and rocky terrain, crossing hollows and a brook without a guide, sensing the upcoming battle. As the first shots were fired by their comrades on the other side of the hill Winston came into his assigned position. He attributed his success to a supernatural power that guided him, blindly, to his assigned post.

On Winston's right, at the northeastern end of the field, the

Major Joseph Winston

King's Mountain

40 **Chapter Five**

South Fork men under Major Chronicle made contact with the Tories. He waved his military hat in the air, getting their attention, then pointed to the hill. He raised the cry "Face the hill." Before he could complete the order a ball struck him down. An aide rushed to help the disabled leader off his horse, placing him on some soft grass to rest. His hand raised slowly, pointing to the hill which his men took as an order to be obeyed at once. The now leaderless South Fork men delivered a hair-raising Indian war cry and attacked the hill with great energy, swearing loudly at the Tories as they went.

On the top of the hill Ferguson began to feel that his situation was becoming a bit precarious. He began to have doubts about the outcome and his thoughts turned to escaping to the protection of Cornwallis, at Charlotte. As the Patriot assault widened on all sides he continued to thin out his men, moving them to the newest threat. As the Patriots gradually brought most of their force to the top, or near the top, of the hill, their deadly fire began to take its toll on the Tory band. Despite a rapid depletion of the ranks, Ferguson's well-trained soldiers would reorganize, close ranks, and when ammunition was gone, initiate a bayonet attack. Chronicle's men drove upward at a furious pace to avenge the loss of their leader. Near the top the Tories let loose a blast that rocked the South Fork Patriots. The attack wavered for a moment, the men were stunned and without an officer they hesitated. An officer from a nearby regiment observed what was taking place, and in the confusion, he rushed in to steady the men, ordered reloading, and directed them to continue their charge, which they did in good fashion.

King's Mountain resembled a volcano of fire, with flashes of gunfire at its base, along its sides, and across the top. The struggle was savage as American fought American on opposite sides. Pent-up hatred burst out on both sides as neighbor fired at neighbor and relative at relative. It was men with hunting caps in a fight to the death with those representing the hated British red coats.

Thomas Young, fighting with Williams, spotted someone shooting with fatal effect from a position in the Tory lines. He scouted around until he could pinpoint the source that was coming from a hollow chestnut tree. The enemy was firing through a knothole in the tree just as you would from a fort. Young sat behind a large rock, braced his long rifle on a log, took careful aim at the target, and fired, placing a single shot through the knothole. The enemy gun was silenced. After the battle he came back to that part of the field and located the old tree that was now battle-scarred. Laying facedown on the ground behind the knothole was a dead soldier. Young turned the body over and came face to face with his younger brother.

Captain Moses Shelby, the young brother to Isaac, was wounded twice. The second wound put him out of the fighting when the bone in one thigh was fractured. Someone helped him down the hill to a little pool of water where he was given a drink from a wooden cup and his shattered thigh was bandaged. It would be three long months before he would be able to stand erect and walk again without the assistance of a cane. Along with several other wounded men he was propped up against the base of a tree to rest. He noticed that a certain soldier was coming back several times for water. On his fourth visit within a half hour Shelby, with his rifle across his legs, said to him in a low, but emphatic voice, "Soldier, if you come back again, I'll shoot you. This is no time to shirk your duty!"

Isaac Shelby's men continued to work their way to the top of the hill only to be forced back by the Tories. At one point his men became entangled with those of Campbell and Sevier as charge and countercharge spread across the side of the hill.

What might have been a victory for the Tories was prevented when Ferguson blew his whistle calling for a retreat to deny the other enemy units from gaining the top of the hill. The militia, being ignorant of the reason for the retreat, became confused and continued to fight. Ferguson's officers were required to shoot some of their own men to have the order carried out.

With the continuing movement of Ferguson's men around the top of the mountain and the success of the Patriots in shooting the enemy, the tide began to shift to the Americans. Patriot units became connected on the slopes and their surge to the top gained momentum. Shelby and Sevier reached the top at about the same time driving the defenders in front of them to the southwest. The two leaders occupied the heel of the open space that resembled a giant shoe sole, with Ferguson's men at the toe end. As the order was given to advance toward the Tories, Campbell's men broke onto the top near them. The three commanders launched an advance, driving toward the enemy camp. As this developed several Tories raised white flags but were promptly cut down by Ferguson and his officers. What remained of the Tory army was trapped. The situation became even more severe as units under McDowell and Cleveland gained the high ground behind the retreating Tories. All efforts to stem the tide with the remaining elements of Ferguson's command failed completely as the heart for fight disappeared. Most were out of ammunition and many had lost their stomach for battle.

Now Ferguson decided it was time to leave the battlefield and his defeated troops, and ride to Charlotte Town. He mounted his horse turning him toward a small opening in the trees that opened to a path down the hill and safety. One hundred feet was all he needed to go, but it was not to be. In his left hand he held his Spanish sword of command engraved with the words:

> Draw me not without reason,
> Sheathe me not without honor.

The battle had lasted one hour and during that time the Patriot soldiers had watched for the British officer. As he mounted his white horse

Chapter Five

and began his ride to the opening, a dozen rifles took aim and fired at short range. As the first bullets pierced his body he raised his sword over his head. Robert Young, of Sevier's command, fired his rifle "Sweet Lips" and the ball struck Ferguson in the face, knocking him off his horse, but he was still alive. (A plain stone marks the spot today.) The frightened horse galloped wildly off, down the side of the mountain and disappeared.

Young James Collins, of Campbell's command, wrote after the battle that Ferguson's body was pierced by no less than fifty bullets. Both of his arms were broken and his hat and clothing had been shredded by Patriot bullets. Around Ferguson lay his men in grotesque heaps.

The hatred between the two forces continued unabated. While some saw the validity of surrendering, others kept up the battle from close range amid the continued confusion.

When their leader fell, the second in command, Captain Abraham dePeyster, raised a flag so high in the air that the mountain men could not help but see it. The officer, in a report to Lord Cornwallis, wrote, "In this situation, the small body of soldiers we had being cut up, and finding it impossible to rally the militia, I thought it proper to surrender as the only means of saving the lives of some of our brave men still left, that they behaved with the greatest gallantry and attention..."

Colonel John Sevier

King's Mountain

Major Joseph McDowell

King's Mountain

The Score Is Settled

The reaction to Ferguson's demise and the white flags was described by Shelby. "It was some time before a complete cessation of firing on our part could be affected. Our men, who had been scattered in the battle, continued to come to the top of the hill and fire, without comprehending in the heat of the moment what was happening, and some who had heard of Buford's fate were willing to follow a bad example."

Shelby did not exaggerate. Despite the growing number of white flags the men continued to fire, raising the shout of "Tarleton's quarter!" It was heard repeatedly as a vicious revenge was executed without remorse by the jubilant Patriots on the doomed Tories.

Shelby rode recklessly among his men, ordering them to stop the slaughter. When within fifteen yards of the enemy he shouted, "If you want quarter, throw down your arms!" They did and the order for them to sit down was given and obeyed by the remaining 800 Tories. The Patriots surrounded the group to stare and taunt.

A victory celebration began with numerous "hurrah for freedom" cheers that lifted from the joyous mountaintop. The victorious Patriots laughed, slapped each other on the back, and danced in jubilation. They did what they had set out to do. They got Ferguson! Amid the happiness and jubilation a shot rang out! Colonel Williams grabbed his chest and fell to the ground from the saddle of his horse. He was attended to at once and carried to a Tory tent to rest.

Thomas Young was near Williams at the time. "The moment that I heard the cry that Colonel Williams was shot, I ran to his assistance for I loved him as a father. They carried him into a tent and sprayed water in his face. He revived and his first words were: 'For God's sake, boys, don't give up the hill!' I left him in the arms of his son, Daniel, and returned to the field to avenge his death."

Most of the mountain men heard the shot but did not know the target. They reasoned only that some bastard Tory had sneaked a final shot at one of their men. In less than a second the Patriots commenced firing into the ring of helpless prisoners. One soldier recorded later that at least one hundred Tories were shot where they sat before Patriot officers brought the slaughter to an

Lord Earl Cornwallis

King's Mountain

President Herbert Hoover visited the King's Mountain battlefield site on October 7, 1930, on the 150th anniversary of the Patriot victory. More than 30,000 were in attendance.

Courtesy Brad Keller

A marker on King's Mountain designating the approximate location where Major Patrick Ferguson's body was riddled with bullets from the "long rifles" of the "over-the-mountain men."

Courtesy Brad Keller

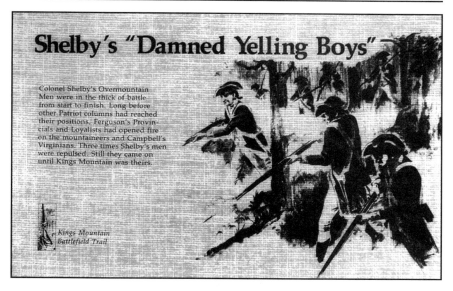

A marker on the grounds of King's Mountain National Military Park, South Carolina. Shelby's men were in the thick of the fighting from start to finish.

Courtesy Brad Keller

end. Colonel Campbell, believing that strict action was called for to control the enemy prisoners, ordered his men to fire. Lieutenant John Hughs recounted the incident years later in filing for his pension. "General Williams was mortally wounded after the British had raised the flag of surrender, by a fire from some of the Tories. Colonel Campbell then ordered a fire on the Tories and we killed nearly a hundred of them...and could hardly be restrained from killing the whole of them."

If Shelby and the others had not acted quickly, more casualties and death would have occurred. He ordered the remaining prisoners to move away from their weapons.

Campbell had second thoughts about his order and went to Shelby the following day to say that he could not account for his conduct during the last of the battle.

One of Shelby's men, James Collins, wrote: "After the fight was over, the situation of the poor Tories appeared to be really pitiable, the dead lay in heaps on all sides, while the groans of the wounded were heard in all directions."

Private William Moore, of Campbell's Virginians, had one of his legs amputated on the field, probably by Dr. Uzal Johnson, of New Jersey. He was left behind in the care of a Patriot home near the battlefield. When his wife in Washington County, Virginia learned of his situation she saddled a horse and rode alone through the mountains during chilly November

Chapter Five

weather to his bedside and nursed him to good health until he was able to ride home.

The Battle of King's Mountain lasted *sixty-five minutes*, and was a total disaster for the British. One-third of Cornwallis' army was lost. Major General Sir Henry Clinton wrote, "No sooner had the news of it spread through the country than multitudes of the disaffected flew to arms from all parts and menaced every British post on both frontiers."

The official report of Shelby, Campbell, and the others to General Horatio Gates stated that Ferguson had 1,125 men on the mountain. Their losses included 19 Provincials killed, 35 wounded, and 68 prisoners for a total of 122. Tory losses were 206 killed, 128 wounded, and 648 prisoners, for a total of 982. The Provincial Corps had one captain killed. The Tories lost two colonels and three captains killed. No one escaped from King's Mountain!

The gallant Patriot army's losses were meager in comparison, suffering only 28 killed and 62 wounded for a total of 90.

In his report on King's Mountain Britain's Lord Rawdon wrote, "A numerous Army now appeared on the Frontiers drawn from the Nolachucki and other Settlements beyond the mountains whose very names had been unknown to us."

Another observation was written by Major George Hanger, briefly attached to Ferguson at one time. "This distinguished race of men are more savage than the Indians, and possess every one of their vices, but not one of their virtues. I have known one of these fellows to travel two hundred miles through the woods never keeping any road or path, guided by the sun by day and the stars by night, to kill a particular person belonging to the opposite party. He would shoot him by his own door and then ride away and boast of what he had done on his return."

Hanger was wrong. The over-the-mountain men were not savages. They were bound together in a common bond to protect their homes and families from names that were well known to them by now. Their leaders had natural ability, tested time and time again in battles with the Indians along the frontier.

Chapter Six

☆☆☆☆☆☆☆☆☆☆☆☆☆☆☆
Away from the Mountain

Worried that Cornwallis or Tarleton might be coming to the aid of Ferguson, Shelby dispatched scouts to search for any evidence of movement. Expecting a fight before they reached home, Shelby knew his men wouldn't have the same adventages as they enjoyed at King's Mountain.

Food was a prime concern the next morning when the army awoke. There was little to eat. Some of Ferguson's provisions, including some wine, were divided among the men. Seventeen captured baggage wagons were stripped of everything which could be carried, and then were burned. Shelby feared that the wagons and prisoners would seriously slow the line of march, placing his men in danger.

The wounded were carried along on hammocks made of blankets and strung between the horses. Branches were cut from the many small saplings on the hillside and made into poles. Blankets were stretched between the poles and fastened. Shelby would not take the Tory wounded, but they would not be treated as Tarleton had treated the Americans. They were not left unattended. Captain dePeyster, in his official report to Lord Cornwallis, said, "Our wounded were left at one Wilsons, four miles this side of the place of action. They are without body clothes or blankets. I fear the man who attends them [is] without medicine and is not sufficiently capable."

As the most seriously wounded were treated it was puzzling to learn that some were men who had fought with Shelby at Musgrove's. When asked why, each gave the same answer that there was no choice. Ferguson told them that they either served him or their homes would be destroyed by fire. Shelby was convinced that they told the truth and so released them. Each was treated as a friend and with respect thereafter.

Also among the prisoners was Virginia Paul, Ferguson's surviving mistress. She was the single "spoils" of the battle that the mountain men ignored. She remained with Shelby's men until they reached Quaker Meadows, and after that there is no record about her.

47

British Responsibility at King's Mountain

Historians note that Cornwallis apparently did nothing to come to the aid of Ferguson's wounded, and how many survived was never recorded. In a letter to his brother after the war he blamed Tarleton for not going to the rescue of Ferguson despite his reported illness. He also alleges that he gave Ferguson orders to avoid any engagement and denied being responsible for the defeat. Cornwallis did not trust Ferguson, yet sent him into the unknown backwoods, an angry, hostile country. Cornwallis gave the orders, but refused to accept the responsibility. Tarleton's writing after the war points an accusing finger at his commanding officer for not sending the British legion to Ferguson's aid. This does not make good military logic. With Tarleton in his sick bed the only other officer who could have been sent was Major George Hanger, who demonstrated his incompetence at Charlotte in front of Cornwallis. In the end with charge and countercharge leveled, the King's Mountain debacle must be laid at the feet of Major Ferguson. His selection of a battle ground was poor and he had the opportunity to escape to Charlotte before the first shot was fired. He failed on both counts.

The prisoners on the march were enlisted to carry most of the 1,200 to 1,500 muskets captured. Only the stronger men carried them, some two and three, all unloaded. Lenoir recorded at least 700 men were used for their transport.

At 10 a.m. Shelby set the column in motion away from King's Mountain. Campbell was left behind to handle the burial detail. He dug two large pits, one for the Patriots and the other for the Tories. The bodies were unceremoniously dumped in, covered, and the work concluded. The letters of Patriot James Collins give a good description of the work: "They were thrown into convenient piles and covered with old logs, the bark of old trees, and rocks, yet not so to prevent them from becoming a prey of the beasts of the forest or the vultures of the air. The wolves [in that area] were so numerous that it was dangerous for anyone to be alone at night for several miles around...also dogs and wild hogs...I saw myself, in passing the place a few weeks after, all parts of the human frame lying scattered in every direction..."

Another account tells that the dead were buried quickly in graves so shallow that wolves were attracted. The wolves and vultures became so bold during their expansive feast that they even attacked people who later came to the site to look for relatives.

Away from the Mountain

> ### Burial Site at King's Mountain
>
> In 1815, on the thirty-fifth anniversary of the battle, residents of the area around King's Mountain gathered up the remaining bones of the dead for a proper burial. Distinguishing Tory from Patriot was impossible. Later, a monument was erected on the site, one side honoring the men who fought with Major Chronicle and the other remembering Ferguson.

As the impatient Shelby got his men moving, the prisoners were lined up in single file with their cargo. When an old man protested that he was too weak to carry the rifles assigned to him, Shelby rode up with a curse, saying he was strong enough to carry one there and he should be strong enough to carry one away. When the old man grumbled under his breath, Shelby slapped him across the shoulder blades with the flat of his sword. The weapons were promptly lifted off the ground and carried away.

The army and its prisoners began a difficult march. Plagued by fever and dysentery and slowed by wounds, it worked its path to the friendly mountains of home in a halting manner, living off pumpkins which the army fried for themselves and gave raw to the prisoners who ate them avidly.

On the first day's march the mountain men covered twelve miles and stopped to rest on a plantation owned by a Tory who owned a large field of sweet potatoes. The footmen who had been left behind at Green River to care for the horses arrived with a most welcomed supply of beef. The famished warriors thus had their first meal of any consequence in three days. Shelby sensed danger in the big meal and the casual air the men now adopted. The next day the army, prisoners and all, estimated at 2,000, covered only three miles. The South Fork men and some South Carolinians broke away from the main body at this point to go home. The command was now a little lighter, but, as Shelby noted, still very short of ammunition should a second fight occur. On October 10, twenty miles were covered and a dozen on the following day, bringing them close to Gilbert Town.

Colonel Campbell asked for a list of the dead and wounded and ordered two hundred men plus officers to be assigned to guard duty each day. Three days later he would issue another order after complaints of the area's inhabitants about plundering parties robbing the homes and farms of Whigs and Tories. He ordered his officers to bring the situation under control.

Food was still in short supply. But, as it was found in small supplies in various places, the fear of pursuit by the British began to fade away. On arrival at a plantation northeast of Gilbert Town, the army decided it was time to carry out their own form of "military justice" on the prisoners.

50   **Chapter Six**

Campbell received formal complaints from several of his junior officers alleging that there were several murderers and house-burners among the prisoners. They asked that a court be convened for their trial and that those who are found guilty be promptly executed before they could escape and commit more crimes against the country.

At this point Shelby reported that an "American officer paroled from Ninety-Six only the day before" arrived in camp, reporting that "he had seen eleven American citizens hung at that place within a few days past, merely for their attachment to the cause of their country."

This account exasperated the officers who were now faced with handling their "trials" with an air of legality, despite the fact that they were extracting revenge and retaliation. Some reasoned that if they put the Tories to the hangman's noose, it would make the British less likely to hang Americans.

There was a visitor in camp at that time and when the "justice" problem arose, the visitor presented to the officers a copy of a new law authorizing two justices of the peace to cause to be apprehended any citizen or Loyalist who might be found in arms against the country, and, if found guilty of treason, to order him to immediate execution without any pleading in the case.

Shelby acknowledged that the army being in Rutherford County, and that there were several county officials present, including the sheriff, the proceeding could go forward. Campbell immediately called a council of officers to try the prisoners and a jury composed of field officers and captains was selected.

The trials began with the "most atrocious offenders" first who had committed murder deliberately in cold blood and destroyed the families of Whigs, burned houses and committed the most enormous crimes." The trials continued until thirty-six had been condemned and sentenced to be hung. At two o'clock the following night the hangings began.

Among those hanged was Ambrose Mills, accused of being one of several Tories present on the occasion of the hanging murder of Noah Hampton. Andrew Hampton, the father, was present as the rope snapped Mills' neck, and the mountain men let loose a cheer. Actually there was no real proof that Mills had anything to do with the murder. So, in the absence of the required evidence, the charge was advanced that Mills had plotted with the Cherokees to ravage the frontier.

Another who expected to perish at the end of the rope at this time was James Crawford. He was identified as a man from the Watauga, who along with Sam Chambers had deserted the mountain men on the way to Gilbert Town and had run to Ferguson's camp with news of the approaching army of mountain men. Chambers was not charged because of his youth. Crawford was allowed to sweat for awhile and then was pardoned at the request of Sevier who had served with him along the frontier against

Away from the Mountain 51

the Cherokees. Sevier pointed out that whatever the intentions of the two deserters, their message to Ferguson had helped "tree the possum on King's Mountain."

Only nine were actually hanged, three at a time. Lieutenant Alshire, an angry witness to the event, recorded that all nine "died like Romans."

The executions were carried out from the projecting limb of an oak tree with the scene illuminated by pine torches. A jubilant Whig was heard to yell that he wished "every tree in the wilderness bore such fruit!" Most of the men had had enough after the first nine. In one instance when the younger brother of a condemned man managed to cut his ropes while pretending to say farewell, not a single shot was fired as the two ran off into the dark forest.

At this point Shelby, Sevier, and Cleveland sensed a change in mood and called a halt to the proceedings. The ropes were removed from the necks of the next three men and the executions came to an end.

As the men disbursed, one of those who had just been pardoned asked for a private meeting with Shelby. He was grateful for the sparing of his life and explained that he was obliged to inform the colonel that Tarleton's army was set to attack the camp at dawn! A woman had come into camp earlier that evening with a message for the British officers to alert them of the attack. The word had been passed to some of the rank and file.

Knowing that Tarleton was a master of the long, hard march and that the report was probably true, he spread the alarm. He wrote later, "The Americans immediately mounted their horses and were ready to march as soon as it was light enough to see, for the night was exceptionally dark. As soon as they could see they started for the mountains." As the march resumed it passed by the nine Tories who were left hanging where their lives had ended.

The rapid movement by the Americans was not lost on their prisoners. DePeyster rode up to Shelby and added to the tension by asking where he was going in such a hurry.

Shelby replied, "To our natural element, the mountains."

"You smell a rat?" dePeyster asked.

"We know all about it," Shelby replied.

Within the first hour of march the rain began to fall, starting slowly and then a steady, heavy downpour, turning the valley into a river. At times the water was waist deep. The goal, to reach the upper Catawba and cross it before Tarleton caught up with them, was still hours away. At 10 p.m. the river came into view and was seen to be rising rapidly. Shelby and Sevier knew time was short, and that a crossing had to be made before it would become impassable.

The prisoners were formed into columns six-wide and told to hold on to each other as if their lives depended on it. By this time the men were completely worn out from nervous exhaustion and hunger. The prisoners

52   **Chapter Six**

had gone without bread and meat for two days, and along the thirty-two mile line of march no less than one hundred had escaped.

The next morning the river had risen to a depth of ten feet and posed a major problem to anyone wishing to cross, including Tarleton. With the wall of water at their back the mountain men felt that "heaven" was now protecting them. Upon reaching Quaker Meadows, the home of Major McDowell, his wooden fences were offered for firewood, and being the last of October and the weather somewhat cold, the suggestion was warmly accepted. One Patriot wrote that "everyone from the command-in-chief to the meanest private was as wet as if he had been dragged through the Catawba River."

The elderly mother of Charles and Joseph McDowell was hostess for a meal that included the British officers who were treated as guests. Her sons recalled that earlier in the summer some of the same officers had been to her home and made threats as to what they would do with her two sons when they caught up with them. Now they were prisoners, cold and disconsolate in the home of the elderly woman they had earlier tormented.

The following day the army rested and reorganized. Then a distressing message arrived. The Cherokees believed that the men were faraway from their homes, and were preparing for numerous attacks. A return to the mountains was now first priority.

Shelby and Sevier conferred. Sevier would take most of their respective commands across the mountains as fast as possible. Shelby would take the prisoners and locate General Gates, or whoever commanded the Continental army, if one still existed, and ask that some action be taken against the Cherokees.

Many of Campbell's Virginians went with Sevier. Campbell remained with the men from Burke, Wilkes, and Surrey Counties under Cleveland, Winston, and McDowell. Now, there were about as many prisoners as mountain men to guard them.

The army pushed forward to the head of the Yadkin, known as Happy Valley. Then, down the Yadkin, past old Fort Defiance, and the site today of Wilkesboro, to the Moravian settlements where Winston-Salem is now situated. Here they learned of the whereabouts of the dreaded Tarleton and Lord Cornwallis who had also suffered from the rains. While the mountain men had struggled with prisoners to escape to the north, pushing their physical endurance to its limits, the British army had been doing the same. It was marching south as fast as it could to escape the "horde of barbarians" that had appeared so suddenly from the mysterious lands of the western waters. A cheer went up at the news that the soil of North Carolina was free of invaders.

As the British ran from the dreadful mountain men, the news of this great victory at King's Mountain spread like wildfire. General Gates, awaiting his removal as Southern commander, sent a courier racing to Governor

Away from the Mountain 53

Thomas Jefferson, of Virginia, with dispatches. Gates termed it a "great and glorious victory." And added, "We are now more than even with the enemy." Jefferson was elated and sent the news on to the Continental Congress where morale was very low. Benedict Arnold had just been exposed and Major John Andre, the spy who had conspired with him, had just been hanged. Two days before the Battle of King's Mountain, General George Washington wrote to his officers, "We have no magazines, nor money to form them and in a little time we will have no men [even] if we had money to pay them. We have lived on expedients until we can live no longer."

Washington's mood and that of Congress changed with the news from Jefferson. Washington wrote that the "news obtained from North Carolina was proof of the spirit and resources of the country." He and the Congress may not have understood the full extent of the victory at King's Mountain, but one year later they would, at Yorktown.

Three South Fork men were indirectly responsible for carrying the news of Ferguson's defeat to Lord Cornwallis. Robert Henry (he fought with the Virginia troops) was wounded in the fighting and was hurting very badly. Two of his friends decided to get him home as soon as possible. This they did without delay. When reaching his family's farm the pain increased and was then treated with a poultice, made of wet ashes, prepared by his mother.

On Monday, the second day after the battle, several people arrived at the Henry house, calling themselves "Neutralists," but in reality were Tories. With great gratification Robert listened as his two friends, Hugh Erwin and Andrew Berry [also with the Virginians], gave their version of the fight.

Tories: It is certain that Ferguson is killed and his army defeated and taken prisoner?

E and B: It is certain for we saw Ferguson dead and his army prisoners.

Tories: How many men had Ferguson?

E and B: Nearly twelve hundred.

Tories: Where did they get men enough to defeat him?

E and B: They had South Carolina and Georgia refugees, Colonel Graham's men, some from Virginia, some from the head of the Yadkin, some from the head of the Catawba and some from over the mountain and some from everywhere else.

Tories: Tell us how it happened.

E and B: We met at Gilbert Town and found that foot soldiers couldn't overtake Ferguson, and we took between six and seven hundred horsemen, having as many or more footmen to follow, and we overtook Ferguson at King's Mountain, where we surrounded and defeated him.

Tories: Ah! That won't do. Between six and seven hundred to surround nearly twelve hundred. It would take more than two thousand to surround and take Ferguson!

54   **Chapter Six**

E and B: But we were all of us Blue Hen's Chickens.

Tories: There must have been of your horse and foot, in all, more than **four thousand!** We see what you are about, that is, to catch Lord Cornwallis napping.

The conversation ended and the "Neutralists" scurried away. Later, neighbors said they had crossed the flooded Catawba by swimming a horse along a canoe and were heading for Charlotte as fast as they could go.

Cornwallis did not accept the first reports of the battle without proper confirmation of such an alleged disaster. According to Shelby, that came several weeks after the battle when Shelby was at General Daniel Morgan's camp at New Providence. There, a respectable, plain-looking old gentleman told the story of being picked up by some of Cornwallis' men and of being questioned by Cornwallis, himself. He was considered a reliable source of information since he had two sons fighting for the Rebels.

"Who defeated Ferguson?" Cornwallis inquired.

"The men from the west under Campbell, Shelby, Sevier and Cleveland," was the reply.

"What is their number and where are they going?"

"My Lord," said the old man with a straightforward, sincere look about his face, "*I understand they are three thousand strong and they are bearing down upon you.*"

Immediately, according to the old man, Cornwallis conferred with his senior officers and thereafter the drums began to beat "to arms," throughout the camp. Within in an hour the British command was on its way south, continuing throughout the night, and in much confusion. When supply wagons broke down from the fierce pace, they were burned on the spot.

A letter written by Lord Rawdon, on behalf of Cornwallis, to General Sir Henry Clinton, on October 29, painted this dark picture: "The defeat of Major Ferguson had so dispirited this part of the country that Lieutenant Colonel Cruger sent information to Earl Cornwallis that the whole district had determined to submit as soon as the rebels should enter it. From these circumstances, from the consideration that delay does not extinguish our hopes in North Carolina, and from the long fatigue of the troops, which made it seriously requisite to give some refreshment to the army, Earl Cornwallis has resolved to remain for the present in a position which may secure the frontiers without separating his forces."

The British were uncertain as to how serious the threat of the backwater men might be at this time. There were other rumors too, of increased numbers joining in with the mountain men who were "bearing down" on Cornwallis. The British commander elected to return to Charleston as quickly as possible, ending his three-pronged thrust through the colonies.

Away from the Mountain 55

Dr. James Thatcher, attached to the Revolutionary Army in the north, wrote the following in his diary on October 20, while at West Point, on the Hudson: "Official intelligence is received of a very brilliant exploit of our militia in North [really South] Carolina. The famous royal partisan, Major Ferguson, was at the head of about one thousand four hundred British troops and tories. Colonels Campbell, Cleveland, Williams, Shelby and Sevier, brave and enterprising officers, had collected detached parties of militia, and by agreement the whole were united, amounting to near three thousand. Colonel Campbell was appointed their commander. They immediately marched in pursuit of Major Ferguson, and came up with him advantageously posted at a place called King's Mountain. No time was lost in making a vigorous attack, and giving the enemy a total defeat, in which Major Ferguson and one hundred and fifty of his men were killed, eight hundred made prisoners, and fifteen hundred stand of arms taken, with trifling loss on our side, excepting the brave Colonel Williams, who received a mortal wound after being crowned with honor."

Isaac Shelby was given full credit for the decisive victory at King's Mountain. He was the instigator of the entire campaign. He shaped it and he drove it! In the coming years many honors would be heaped upon him and many towns and counties would bear his name. In the later stages of his life he would seldom refer to his many additional enormous achievements, but was most proud of that day at King's Mountain when a British monster was eliminated by an army of American mountain men.

John Sevier raced his men across the mountains, stopping at his home in Washington County (North Carolina), just long enough to kiss his bride and learn the happy news that she was pregnant. Pushing on to Washington County, Virginia, he joined with Arthur Campbell, a cousin of William Campbell and a neighbor of Sevier, to defeat a small army of Cherokees on the Tennessee River. While there they burned more than one thousand homes, took an estimated five thousand bushels of corn, and forced the Cherokees into a treaty. Taken from a dead Indian was a pouch containing papers with positive proof that the British were behind the Cherokee raids.

Chapter Seven

✩✩✩✩✩✩✩✩✩✩✩✩✩✩✩

Other Duties

Isaac Shelby was delegated to offer a number of mountaineers who were anxious to serve under General Daniel Morgan to General Gates, now in his last weeks as commander of the Southern forces. Shelby spent November with Morgan himself in the Continental army headquarters at New Providence, South Carolina, while waiting for Gates to return to camp.

Daniel Morgan was a rugged old man who, during the French and Indian War, survived 499 lashes given by a British officer. He often took off his shirt to show the ugly, distorted flesh marks to his soldiers before a battle. He also suffered greatly from piles, rheumatism, sciatica, malaria hangovers and other recurring ailments, but he was always ready for a fight.

Shelby had some suggestions for Morgan, one of which was to take a force of men and drive the British out of Fort Ninety-Six, the source, he believed, for the British to arm and incite the Cherokees to wage war against the settlers.

Upon Gates' return the two sat on a pair of tree stumps and conferred. The reasoning was sound and Gates agreed to take action. The following morning the two rode to Charlotte Town to ask the North Carolina War Board for the necessary militia for General Morgan. The board agreed and Shelby then departed for home after promising to return in the spring with three hundred riflemen. As he rode out on the trail he passed Nathaniel Green who was to relieve Gates of his command.

Morgan set out on the road to Ninety-Six to implement Shelby's plan and was followed closely by a strong British force of 1,000 selected soldiers, under Tarleton, with orders from Cornwallis to destroy the Americans. For two nights Morgan stayed hours ahead of the enemy, then he stopped running at Cowpens and made camp. As expected Tarleton struck at first light, but Morgan had set a trap. The British ran into a first line of mostly green troops who, as ordered, fired two shots point-blank range into the redcoats' front line felling many men and officers. The first line

Other Duties **57**

retreated, as ordered by Morgan, to a second with similar orders. On came Tarleton, believing he had won the day as the Patriots fled before him. The second line repeated the damage of the first, then got out of the way to allow a strong line of regular Continental soldiers, hidden by the rise in a hill, to slam into the surprised British. Behind this line came the thundering hooves of Morgan's best cavalry.

Morgan's plan worked to perfection and resulted in one of the most spectacular victories of the war. Tarleton was completely embarrassed and in one stroke, fully one-third of Cornwallis' field army was lost, including his best cavalry. In this "upset," Morgan had successfully pulled off the impossible. He had used untried troops against British cavalry charges and had won.

Cornwallis would later write that, "The late affair [at Cowpens] broke my heart." Mustering what he could of two thousand men he vowed to follow the American army, under its new commander General Nathanael Greene, to the end of the world. That turned out to be Guilford Court House, North Carolina, in March of 1781, where he won the battle but lost another fourth of his men to General Greene. The battle was the second bloodiest since Bunker Hill. The dead and dying lay for two days under heavy rains while both sides tried to sort them out. Thereafter, Cornwallis, with his army greatly reduced, limped toward Wilmington.

In March, with information that the Cherokee were not abiding by the treaty, Shelby put together a small army and marched toward Tennessee. Along the way he obtained intelligence from scouting parties of friendly Indian tribes. After several days' march they came upon the Chickamauga towns where they set everything to the torch that had not been burned earlier. The treaty that had been delayed due to the violations was reset for July. Isaac and his father were named commissioners.

An earlier request to Shelby from General Greene to furnish a company of riflemen for pursuit of the British was now impossible and Shelby deeply regretted it. Greene managed to keep pressure on the British and on June 25 took Augusta. In this action Moses Shelby took part, acting as captain, while still recovering from thirteen saber wounds at Cowpens.

Another appeal was issued to Isaac Shelby from Greene to come to his aid at Fort Ninety-Six. Greene had the fort within his grasp until late-arriving British reinforcements intervened. He begged Shelby to come at once to drive the enemy back into the southern sections.

As the crops were planted and the treaty was null and void, he quickly raised 500 riflemen and John Sevier another 200. As word came that the British had retreated to Orangeburg and maybe even to Charleston, Shelby dispatched the following letter to Greene: "...that distance being so very great for us, the warm season of the year, and the men not prepared for a long Tower, has induced Col. Sevier of this county and myself from proceeding on our march...the men are ordered to hold themselves in readiness to march on the shortest notice."

Chapter Seven

A second letter of some urgency, written by Greene to Shelby, took one month to reach its destination in the Holston. It urged Shelby and the man to come at once as he suspected Cornwallis would return from Virginia with reinforcements. Intercepting his lordship, Greene wrote, could put a finishing touch to the war.

Seven hundred men answered the call, most in twenty-four hours, for another sixty days and marched off to administer a "finishing touch" to his lordship. Isaac Shelby's brother, Evan, Jr., also signed on.

Days before Shelby's men were to arrive in Charlotte Town, where they were to receive orders, news came that Cornwallis was not on his way south, rather, that he had been trapped in the small Virginia village of Yorktown and had surrendered to General Washington, as British musicians played "The World Turned Upside Down."

Chapter Eight

☆☆☆☆☆☆☆☆☆☆☆☆☆☆☆

Monck's Corner, November 1781; A Return to Farming

The militia refused to go home, saying that if it was not permitted to get at Cornwallis then they certainly should be allowed to fight the British and put the final strokes on the American victory. They joined Greene about fifty miles from Charleston but found that fodder for their horses was in very short supply. Greene immediately sent them forward another eighty miles to the camp of Francis Marion, the "Swamp Fox." A quiet man, Marion was one of the Revolution's most colorful figures, a guerrilla leader whose men often lived on nothing more than sweet potatoes, snake meat, and swamp water laced with vinegar. Between long periods of Bible reading, he led his followers on deadly strikes against the British, appearing out of thin air and vanishing the same way. Greene advised Marion that the mountain men were equal to any task and that if he wanted to keep them, he would have to keep them busy.

A British outpost at Monck's Corner occupied Marion's attention, and he planned an expedition against it to include Shelby and his men. Shelby was surprised to learn that he would be second in command, assuming that he would direct the attack because most of the men were his command from North Carolina and besides, he outranked the South Carolina officer who had been given the command. Isaac refused to march, and was supported by his men.

His 500 mountain men rested uneasily when Marion rode to Shelby and asked his reason for not marching. Isaac explained and was told by Marion that the other officer was selected because he knew the country. Marion did not. Immediately Isaac consented to participate. He later told friends that he decided it was best to go along because "...in the short time I was to stay in the camp I thought Marion to be so much a gentleman and he so treated me. Indeed, throughout the expedition he gave me no orders but consulted me on all occasions."

After two days' travel on narrow and very obscure paths, through wooded and swampy ground, the party arrived at the Monck's Corner

59

60   **Chapter Eight**

post, held by the Hessians. Patriots along the way advised Shelby and Marion that the fort was anxious to capitulate to the Americans and there would be no resistance. However, when an officer went inside the fort with a demand for its surrender, the garrison officer replied that the post would be defended to the death.

Shelby himself then went in and carefully explained what would happen if the fort resisted and how the battle would end. He questioned whether the garrison could standoff his troops storming it. "If you do, he said, then rest assured that each and everyone of you will be put to the sword." Shelby pointed out very deliberately that he had many men, armed with guns and tomahawks, just awaiting the opportunity to fall upon them.

The officer in charge asked if Shelby had any artillery, to which the reply was yes. "We have enough guns," he said, "to blow your post to toothpicks and every man of you to hell!"

The officer surrendered.

Writing about the incident at the fort later, Isaac said it appeared to him that it could have been held with the men stationed there, especially since the Patriots *do not have artillery!* And secondly because there was a second British fort only 500 yards away that was not under siege. This came to light as they advanced toward it and suddenly found themselves surrounded by 150 cavalry. Shelby wheeled the men around and prepared to advance, but the soldiers from the other fort surrendered, not having the will to fight.

A return to Marion's camp was started at once, taking along what captured supplies they could manage and those prisoners who were able to make the sixty-mile trek. Upon arriving on the Santee River they learned that what remained of the entire British army was in an old field and only three miles distant. Shelby was given the assignment to advance upon the redcoats and to attack if the enemy advanced, or retreated, using his discretion. His men rapidly advanced and to their delight saw the British retreat in confusion, tossing their knapsacks, canteens and guns aside as they ran. They did not stop running until reaching Charleston.

With this action, Shelby and Sevier had boxed in the only remaining British force in the South. On November 25, the 60-day enlistments of his men expired and they started for home, with the last miles being covered with deep snow. Elected to the North Carolina legislature Shelby waited three days, then he began his trip north to Salem.

The Revolutionary War came to an end in the South during the spring and summer of 1782. Shelby was active in the state legislature, being re-elected in the spring. When the lawmakers adjourned, he rode back to the Holston and hearing of more Indian troubles, prepared for an expedition against the Chickamaugas. The planned effort was called off when Virginia and North Carolina announced that they were out of funds.

During the summer Isaac Shelby was named one of three commissioners appointed by North Carolina to survey the lands along the Cumberland River near what is today Nashville, Tennessee. That land was given to officers in the Revolutionary War, including Isaac's brothers, Moses and Evan. As the year 1782 came to an end, he turned his thoughts to Kentucky and settling down on a peaceful land. However, he would continue to play an important role in the struggle to build an independent nation, free of foreign domination.

Chapter Nine

☆☆☆☆☆☆☆☆☆☆☆☆☆☆☆
Kentucky's First Governor

Shelby was saddened by news from Kentucky. His friend, Nathaniel Hart, with whom he had shared a keen interest in that state, was reported killed by Indians. His party was ambushed within a short distance of the Hart fort at White Oak Spring. Hart was knocked from his horse and scalped while his daughter Susannah watched.

There were many Indian attacks against the white settlements throughout 1782. Mutilated white corpses could be seen floating down the Ohio River past other settlements, raising great alarm. In August British rangers led a series of raids along with the Indians. One was a siege against the Hart fort that lasted for three weeks, during which time the hundred settlers, crowded inside its narrow space, did not change clothing at night for fear of an attack. Another attack was against Bryant's Station lasting twenty-four hours during which it was bombarded with bullets and arrows. The raids produced rage among the settlers who formed a force of 185 men, caught up with the attackers at Lower Blue Licks, engaging them for a short time with disastrous results. More than sixty Kentucky men and boys were shot to death and scalped.

As winter began the British signed away their rights to the northwestern posts and in the south the Indians were soundly defeated along the Miami River. Although the warring was now over, the Kentuckians were without this knowledge and continued battle preparations.

In October 1782 Isaac Shelby left the Holston territory for Kentucky, accompanied by his cousin, John Shelby, Jr., thirty years old. He was to buy land for himself and other Shelby family members. They were accompanied along the Wilderness Trail by three slaves and several others. They visited with the Harts, and then moved on to Knob Lick where Isaac built a cabin. This spot would later serve as the family graveyard.

During the summer of 1783 Isaac married Susannah Hart. He was thirty-two and she was nineteen. Little is known of the occasion or the

Kentucky's First Governor

celebration that must have followed. After planting a number of crops in the spring Isaac cleared more than 200 acres of land and began planning for a large home. At Isaac's invitation, his brother James began a journey to Kentucky where he also owned some land. However, he and his party were intercepted and killed by a band of roving Indians at Crab Orchard Springs, less than twenty miles from Isaac's home. About a year later, in 1785, Isaac and Susannah welcomed their first born, a son, who was named after James. Less than a year later Susannah's mother, Sarah Simpson Hart, died. On the birth of their next child, a daughter, she was named Sarah Simpson Shelby.

Isaac and his brothers became greatly disturbed at recent news from North Carolina that their father, Evan, was courting very heavily a woman many years his junior, who was considered a brash golddigger. Their feelings were confirmed when they learned that Isabella Elliott had demanded that one-third of his estate be deeded to her before she would accept his marriage proposal.

Evan Shelby, though advanced in years, and unwise in affairs of the "heart," was involved in a most interesting adventure at this time. Most of his land holdings were in Washington County, Virginia, which bordered on Sullivan County and Green Counties in North Carolina. These three counties joined together to form a separate state named "Franklin," and were waiting for their application for admission to the Union to be approved. Evan Shelby approved the action and even supported its independent operations. The separation question had produced a near state of civil war with reports of gunshots among the residents. Shelby then became a leader in the opposition and came down in opposition to Isaac's great friend and military commander John Sevier, a separation leader, who became the first governor of Franklin. Finally, North Carolina reached out to the three counties whose main complaint was about the absence of any military protection, incorporated them into another district named Washington, and in 1787 Evan was named brigadier general of the area. Later the same year, at the age of seventy, Evan married his young heartthrob, and when their first son was born he was named James.

When Sevier's term expired as governor of Franklin, the Franklin assembly named Evan to succeed him, but he refused. Evan also resigned his military post. The state of Franklin went out of existence in 1789 and its territory reverted to North Carolina. Later, in 1796 it was incorporated into the state of Tennessee. (John Sevier served seven terms as governor.) Evan eventually retired to private life and fathered two more children.

It is interesting that at the same time Evan was considering marriage and was being promoted for governor, Isaac was becoming caught up in the question of statehood for Kentucky. The residents maintained a close eye on the proceedings in North Carolina as they debated among themselves their hope for eventual separation from Virginia.

Chapter Nine

After three years, in 1786, Isaac finished building his home, a very large one, and called it "Traveler's Rest." As construction was underway the land was still in Virginia. Years later when visitors to his Kentucky home would ask where all of the stones had come from, he would joke "from Virginia!" Actually, the Shelby home was one of the first five or six homes to be built on the new land of Kentucky. (It weathered four generations until being accidentally burned in 1905. The owner tried to smoke out a wasp's nest between the roof and the chimney. Within its ashes was found the date stone upon which Isaac had carved his name and the completion date a century before. It was set in the walls of the rebuilt home a year later.)

Isaac Shelby became highly involved in state duties at Frankfort. Prior to his first term as governor he and Susannah had their fourth and fifth children. Thomas Hart Shelby, born in 1789, and Susannah Hart Shelby, born in 1791. They developed a large and well-managed plantation with numerous crops and cattle. Continually interested in improving crops and ways to farm, he lent his energies to support of the Kentucky Society for the Promotion of Useful Arts. It encouraged agricultural education, and the distribution of information about good farming and breeding. Shelby helped to organize it and served as its first president.

Kentucky began to change very rapidly. More and more of the original pioneers and settlers were being pushed out as thousands of new people moved in onto small plots of land, slaughtering the animals, and bringing business and light industry. Properties owned by "tomahawk" rights yielded to the surveyor's maps and lawyer's arguments. While there were remaining "thanks" to the valiant efforts of men like Daniel Boone who had opened up the area for settling, the "newcomers" now thought the coonskin cap a novelty.

Isaac Shelby had shed his ties forever with North Carolina when he settled in Kentucky and built his home. Actually the name "Kentucky" did not exist anymore. It had been Kentucky County, a division of the larger Fincastle County named after the house of her Virginia governor, the earl of Dunmore. In 1780 it was divided into three counties: Fayette, Jefferson, and Lincoln. Each of these would subdivide in the next ten years as the population rapidly increased. Shelby's home at Knob Lick was in Lincoln County, Virginia.

Serious problems arose as the seat of the Virginia government was at Williamsburg and later at Richmond. Laws passed were not always applicable to the frontier and more often inadequate overall. Protection of the frontier was impossible. Indian raids could not be countered unless permission was obtained from the state capital and the governor's office. This required a long-distance ride to and from the capital over dangerous trails and always too late to be of any use.

Kentucky's First Governor
65

Eventually a call went up for a Kentucky Convention. Men assembled in Danville on December 27, 1784, representing the militia companies of each Kentucky community. Isaac Shelby was elected chairmen of this first of ten conventions, with delegates elected at large. In 1785 the convention petitioned the Virginia assembly for separation and in January of the following year a separation enabling act was approved allowing the area to become a state in the Confederation of States.

An argument was made in several conventions that Kentucky become a completely independent country. The argument was carried forward by a former Revolutionary War general, James Wilkinson. The Union's foot dragging on the statehood matter was to blame. Wilkinson argued that it took seven conventions by Kentucky, while waiting for word, and that was about all he could stand. The *Kentucky Gazette,* Kentucky's first newspaper, was organized to act as a forum for statehood and separation from Virginia. But debates started endorsing secession from the Confederation of States.

Wilkinson continued to push hard for his cause. Despite hard feelings toward the Spanish for having pirated Kentucky's very first shipment of goods to the Deep South, he met in secret with the Spanish governor of New Orleans, swore a secret alliance with Spain, and returned to Kentucky loaded down with goods, including gold and slaves. While with the Spanish governor, Wilkinson had vowed that Kentucky was ready to become independent and asked for money to be distributed among several dozen Kentucky leaders as a bribe for bringing about its independence. The plan failed.

Finally, in 1790, in its ninth convention, terms for separation were accepted. In February of 1791, the new national legislature of the United States of America authorized Kentucky's admission as the fifteenth state. Isaac was named a delegate to the tenth and final convention which met to determine the structure of the new state's constitution. All free white males of twenty-one years or older and residents of the state could vote. There would be no religious or property requirements to qualify. A bill of rights established further freedoms; however, there was no provision made for public education as provided by its neighboring states of North Carolina and Georgia. In heated arguments within the conventions, the clergy and its sympathizers had won over the landowners, including Isaac Shelby.

The state constitution called for an executive, legislative, and judicial branch. The governor and senate were to be selected by electoral vote while members of the lower house would be chosen by popular vote.

Over the next two years Indian problems persisted. The federal government was not able to provide adequate protection to the citizens of its newest state. The Kentucky militia was ordered into readiness by the secretary of war. For reasons unknown, the militia was allowed to stand down while rumors of Indian attacks and atrocities swirled about. Then, the

Chapter Nine

militia was dismissed as suddenly as it was called to duty. Its members hardly had time to make the readjustment when it was called again to join General Harry Harmar and General John Hardin to attack Indian villages in the northwest along the Scioto River. The majority of the militia balked, not wanting to be guided by non-Kentuckian officers whom they suspected knew nothing about fighting the Indians. Eventually, the militia was persuaded to make the attack which proved to be a complete disaster. Court-martials were immediately instigated against the officers. The militia revolted at the incompetence of the regular army. Determined to form its own army, they demanded that Isaac Shelby be one of its leaders.

President George Washington, in April of 1791, named a five-man Federal War Board for the defense of Kentucky that included Isaac Shelby, Benjamin Logan, John Brown, and Harry Innes. The regular army troops were consolidated with a large number of recruits and volunteers to again attack the tribes along the Scioto River. General Arthur St. Clair, a Revolutionary War soldier who was placed in command, overruled the objections of the five-man board. St. Clair who was gout-ridden required his staff to assist him in mounting his horse.

Kentuckians left the ranks in great numbers as their six-month's service period ended, and many didn't wait that long. Simon Kenton elected to not serve under St. Clair. It wasn't that he disliked the man, rather that he had serious reservations about his ability to fight the fierce Indians. Kenton, a veteran Indian fighter, had fought under men of little military or Indian fighting ability and the results were generally bad.

The general had little knowledge of Indian warfare and ignored Washington's advice to hire good scouts. When reaching a position within four miles of the border dividing Ohio and the Indian territory on November 3, he established a camp and settled in to await supplies and elected to wait until morning to erect fortifications. St. Clair did send some militia and a ranger unit to establish a forward post. More than three thousand Indians were waiting.

At dawn of the next day, November 4, several skirmishes were reported but the alarm was not sounded. St. Clair had his men up early, and while complaining of pain from his gout-afflicted feet, he addressed his men. He ordered the immediate erection of fortifications, brought up the artillery, and ordered the men to come under arms. St. Clair hardly had finished uttering the orders when the bushes and shrubs burst open with screaming Indians attacking and catching the crude camp off guard. The first burst of fire from the army was effective and momentarily stalled the attackers. Only two cannon fired one round each with no apparent damage inflicted. Then, the camp was overrun with warriors, knifing, shooting, and scalping the soldiers.

When this attack ended, more than 900 men were killed or captured by braves of Chiefs Little Turtle and Blue Jacket. It was the largest number of Americans to ever be massacred by the Indians. News of the loss reverberated throughout the frontier as every outpost expected to be overrun by the Indians at any moment.

St. Clair's army, with all of its tribulations, dissension, dissatisfaction, and supply problems, had another problem from within. Unknown to its officers and men there was one particular twenty-three-year-old Kispokotha Shawnee named Tecumseh, who was a spy for the Indian confederation. He regularly sent runners to the north with information about the army's strength and weaknesses, providing the Indian chiefs with the intelligence they needed.

In June of the following year, 1792, some raids on Indian villages were successful, including one led by Isaac Shelby against the Chickamauga towns on the southern boundary of Kentucky. Another raid was made against the Indian territory along the Tippecanoe.

Following the completion of the Kentucky Convention, as reported in *The Kentucky Gazette,* the electors from the different counties in the new state cast ballots naming a new governor and senate. Issac Shelby, Esq. was named the first governor. Isaac had done very little to promote his election having had in abundance the qualities most imperative for this highest position. The most conspicuous quality being his leadership and military record. He kept the electors in suspense for several days before accepting the position. Then on June 4, 1792, at the age of forty-one, the same day that Kentucky officially became the fifteenth star in the new nation's flag, he was inaugurated. To add to this great honor, in the same month Shelby County was created out of Jefferson County and Shelbyville was named its county seat, all in his honor.

Much work lay ahead as the new state took its place with its companions, but Isaac faced it straight on. A touch of irony occurred on the day he was sworn into office. Even while he was giving his acceptance speech, at the far end of town, within sight of some of those attending, a band of renegade Indians conducted a raid killing a number of his fellow Kentuckians.

The first permanent Kentucky State House, at Frankfort, was constructed between 1793 and 1794. It was destroyed by fire on November 25, 1813. Governor Shelby served, beginning in 1792.
Courtesy *An Historical Atlas of Kentucky and her Counties*

The second permanent Kentucky State House, at Frankfort, was built between 1814 and 1816. It, too, was destroyed by fire on November 4, 1824. Governor Shelby would have served here from 1812 to its burning.
Courtesy *An Historical Atlas of Kentucky and her Counties*

Chapter Ten

☆☆☆☆☆☆☆☆☆☆☆☆☆☆

The First Term

Isaac Shelby presided over the first official session of the Kentucky legislature just two days after his inauguration. He initiated action on the establishment of public and private credit, the speedy settlement of land disputes, election laws, requirements that public officials post bond for the performance of official duties, and laws compelling proper treatment of slaves.

The session lasted twelve days and each representative was paid the sum of one dollar a day. Isaac's annual salary was set at about $1,000. He was paid in animal skins or silver coins, weighed and cut into bits.

The new state treasurer's bond was about one-half million dollars, even though the first year's revenue was only $16,400. Kentucky's judicial system was established next; then military divisions were set up making all males between eighteen and forty-five years of age eligible for military duty. Exceptions were ministers, college professors and certain others.

The design of a state seal was next in order. The finished product depicted two male friends in an embrace. Above them was the single word, *Kentucky.* Below, *United we stand, Divided we fall.* Shelby's personal papers attribute the state seal design to a James Wilkinson.

As the year 1792 came to an end a state capital was selected from among several communities that had offered money and other considerations for the honor. Eventually the selection was narrowed down to either Lexington or Frankfort. The selection committee picked Frankfort by a single vote and caused some hard feelings in many corners of the state. Shelby had little to do with the outcome but did approve of the choice. Shortly after the selection he moved his family to the new capital from his beloved Traveler's Rest.

Shelby's first year in office witnessed unsettled relations with the Indians. There were unsuccessful raids into Ohio country and Indian attacks continued inside Kentucky. At Frankfort, guards fought Indians attacking the workers building the capital building. In January of 1793, Isaac's younger

69

Chapter Ten

brothers Evan and Moses were in a party attacked by a large Indian raiding party. Evan Shelby III, at age 39, was killed. Moses escaped unhurt. The attack came very close to the home Evan had built for his wife and young child in Montgomery County, Tennessee.

As Indian troubles gradually settled down, other problems arose. The French had fought with the Americans as the struggle for independence was being bitterly waged. Now, France faced off against England and Spain and many Americans sided with their former comrade. The governor of Virginia considered leaving his post to accept a position in the French army. Isaac was counted among the pro-French supporters.

The Frenchman, Edmund Genet, turned his attention to Spanish possessions along the Mississippi. His earlier travels through Kentucky had sharpened his senses to French sympathies existing there. He sent four French agents into the state to put together an armed group that might aid in his plans. A military leader immediately stepped forward by the name of George Rogers Clark. He was named major general in the armies of France and commander in chief of the Revolutionary legions on the Mississippi. A close friend of Isaac's from earliest pioneering and frontier days, Ben Logan joined with Clark. Thereafter, Kentuckians in numbers volunteered to join Clark and Genet in combat to take Louisiana away from the Spanish and turn it over to France.

President Washington became alarmed on hearing of the planned action and at once wrote a letter to Shelby with his concerns. He feared a rupture of relations with the Spanish over American rights to travel and trade on the Mississippi, possibly leading to a war. Shelby replied instead to Thomas Jefferson, a well-known admirer of the French. He expressed his opinion that he had no jurisdiction in this matter and could not prevent private citizens who were arming themselves from leaving the state, pointing out that there was no law at that time in either case. Thereafter, Washington issued a proclamation warning citizens against taking arms against a nation at peace with the United States. He also ordered General Anthony Wayne to stop all movement of any parties down the Ohio River to attack Spanish territory. The plot against the Spanish failed when Genet was recalled to France during a change in government which disavowed his actions. Genet, perhaps mindful of the fact that he might risk losing his head on return to his native land, elected to stay in the United States. He eventually married the wealthy daughter of the governor of New York.

One of the most popular successes of Shelby's first term was the opening of the vastly improved "Wilderness Trail," called "Shelby's Wilderness Trail" by many historians. The "Trail" had been only a rough path from the early days of Daniel Boone. Conditions improved immediately when the federal postal route used the trail. Later, the postal service switched to the Ohio River, but through Shelby's influence, it returned to the trail. As Kentucky had no money to improve the trail, Isaac was

The First Term 71

successful in getting more than 100 citizens to pledge donations and in 1792 the improvements began. Militia was authorized to guard the traffic that was rapidly increasing. The improvements continued off and on for several years, section by section. It became clearly marked and safe as emigration heightened. But, eventually with the rapidly increasing heavy traffic, further improvement of its surfaces was demanded for heavy-laden wagons and thousands of hearty pioneers. This required leaving the original, rough path that had been pioneered by Boone in many places.

As his first term neared an end he could look back on a successful period. The state's finances were in good shape, the judicial and governmental systems were sound, and Kentucky's borders were safe. He had the good fortune to name good men to high government posts and their performances added to the luster of his first term.

The term of office had its sorrowful moments, including the death of his brother, Evan, and that of his father, Evan Shelby, Sr. He was named executor of his father's estate and carried the responsibility to his last years. In 1814 his father's estate was sold to James King, who had fashioned the headstone for his father's grave and who was owner of the Holston Iron Works and after whom Kingsport, Tennessee is named. The settlement, although considered to have been founded by his father, became known as King's Meadows.

Isaac's seventh child was born on May 30, 1795 and was named after him. His last day of his first term of governor was June 7, 1796. It was time to return to Traveler's Rest and its abundant land. At last he was free of Indian wars and intrusions and politics. He refused to run for a second term despite numerous urgings. He also turned down a nomination to the state senate, but did act as a republican elector in the national elections, supporting Thomas Jefferson in 1801 and 1805, James Madison in 1809, and James Monroe in 1817.

Shelby's land holdings in the early 1800s amounted to more than six thousand acres in Lincoln, Fayette, Clark and Shelby Counties. Shelby's farm was one of the best cattle-producing farms in the state in the 1820s, selling up to forty per year, on average. He kept detailed notes on lineage and was a leader in breeding through the Society for Promoting Useful Arts. Beside his huge beef herds, the farm was home to numerous sheep, horses, pigs, mules, and deer. This was of great benefit at a time when money was almost nonexistent and barter was king. The Shelby farm also included several tenant farmers, several white indentured servants, an overseer, some twenty adult slaves and numerous slave children. He was always charitable toward his slaves and according to family history, Harriet Beecher Stowe spent much time in Kentucky before writing her antislavery novel, *Uncle Tom's Cabin*. In that book, the good master named Shelby, is named after Isaac. Many of his slave families named their children after him in honor of their admiration for him.

Chapter Ten

Another major production of the Shelby farm was whiskey, producing about two thousand gallons a year in addition to thousands of gallons more of cider and apple brandy. In 1811 he marked his 61st birthday. Many honors had come to him since departing his home in western Maryland. He had performed outstanding service to his country and his state and had been honored by each. His residence at Traveler's Rest was visited often by people of all walks of life, including war veterans seeking advise and occasionally money. He was always generous with both. The following year would see his country ask again for his services. And again he would answer the call.

Chapter Eleven

Answering the Call as the Bloodletting Begins

The 1812 election for governor featured a popular and charismatic friend of Shelby's, Gabriel Slaughter. Friend or not, Slaughter thought he should see what Isaac's thoughts were on the political front. Was he contemplating running? Would he stay on the sideline this time and lend his support? If anyone could bolster his campaign, it was Isaac. But, Isaac declined. Only, he said, if there came a national emergency and his leadership and experience were needed. Satisfied, Slaughter proceeded with his campaign.

The infant and indigent United States wanted no part of the warring between France and England. The British blockade of the eastern shoreline and the impressment of sailors from eastern-bound commerce into its navy did not weigh on the minds of Kentuckians. If anything, the fear was of an Indian-British cooperation restarting savage attacks with arms supplied to the Indians by the English. Tecumseh, the brilliant Shawnee leader, was on a mission to the tribes strung out between Florida and Canada, urging an alliance against the white man's consistent augmentation westward. His rumored successes irritated the settlers and governments, conjuring up dark war clouds again.

The Kentucky voters in 1810 approved Henry Clay and Richard M. Johnson, men who supported war, if necessary. Clay preached the capture of British Canada by the Kentucky militia. This would, he said, protect the white frontier. Johnson agreed and volunteered to go with the militia. This fervor branded Clay and Johnson as "war hawks" in Washington.

The issue was joined in the fall of 1811 when the Prophet, brother of Tecumseh, broke Tecumseh's orders to maintain the peace on the fragile frontier. His raids brought immediate reaction. Indiana Governor William Henry Harrison gathered a militia at Vincennes that included many from Kentucky and a federal regiment. The Battle of Tippecanoe erupted on November 7, when more than six hundred Indians hurled themselves at Harrison's camp at night. Harrison's men managed to fend off the attack,

74   Chapter Eleven

sustaining about three dozen casualties. The Indian settlement was burned and in it was discovered British guns and powder. This action drove the Indians closer to the British, but consolidated the hatred of both by the frontier settlements. For Harrison the fruits of this victory made him the top man on the list of men the Kentuckians wanted to lead them in war.

France and England began to close the noose around the colonies thus preventing trade with any country. American ships were confined to its shoreline by very strict regulations, and America debated its future. Side with the French, or the British? Finally, war was declared against London. And on July 14, 1812, less than one month before the election, Isaac Shelby announced that he would run for governor of Kentucky. This was in response to an avalanche of letters and personal appeals. He would answer his country's call for help.

The campaign between Isaac and Slaughter, who was now a bit miffed about his friend's decision, was short. Isaac represented the Jeffersonian Republican Party, although, unlike today, the distinction was blurred. Candidates, to all appearances, were above it all. The battle, or mud sling-ing for votes was waged by subordinates. Detractors called attention to his age of 62 years with the sobriquet "Old Daddy Shelby." There were fist fights, catcalls and more at rallies. His most devout supporters de-clared that they wanted "Old King's Mountain" for governor. This too gave birth to political attack by his enemies who were quoted in a Ken-tucky newspaper that "Isaac had run at King's Mountain!"

Raising the temper of the old fighter, he angrily refuted the charges in several newspaper articles. While his friends knew very well of his leadership at King's Mountain, those not familiar with the epic battle were confused. However, the first governor's popularity weathered the storm and he was elected with 29,285 votes to Slaughter's 11,936. Kentucky was now on a war footing and Shelby was ready to act.

The 2,000 Kentuckians who volunteered in June to help General Wil-liam Hull take Canada assembled at Georgetown. They were signing up at the same time Hull was surrendering Fort Detroit without a shot, hav-ing been driven off Canadian soil by the Indians. He was later sentenced to be hanged for cowardice, although he would be reprieved for earlier bravery. News of the surrender put the brakes on the Kentuckians before they had gone as far as the Ohio River. The threat of Indian warfare loomed again along the entire frontier. Now came the question. If the war was to proceed, who would lead the forces? Kentuckians wanted the victor at Tippecanoe, William Henry Harrison.

Harrison was visiting in Frankfort along with some of the state's leading citizens, including Henry Clay and Governor Scott. Two days be-fore his second inauguration, Shelby met in Frankfort with Harrison and Scott and it was settled. Indiana Governor Harrison would be named gen-eral of the Kentucky militia. This would bypass the state constitution that provided for the state militia to be commanded by a Kentuckian. For the

Answering the Call as the Bloodletting Begins 75

good of the country, Shelby agreed to give Harrison command of his militia along with those of Indiana and Illinois. President James Madison then appointed Harrison as commander of the Northwestern army.

Shelby's first act as governor was to order several regiments into position to help defend the territories of Illinois and Indiana. More troops were organized to send to Harrison and another 2,000 were called up to attack the Indians along the Wabash to increase Harrison's chances of recapturing Detroit. In these first few months no less than 7,000 Kentuckians went off to battle and many were turned away from service. While the state warmed to its patriotic passions, the harsh realities of war came home to those in the Northwest as winter dropped its white blanket of snow over the landscape.

The volunteers on the Wabash ran out of provisions within six days. The officers found discipline difficult to establish and when the Indians fired the prairie grasses, taking feed from the horses, and threatening their very lives with a horrible death, they turned for home. The men voted to go back without having faced the enemy, a gross disappointment to Shelby.

Meanwhile Harrison was making headway despite being reduced to half-rations and heavy rains, requiring that he wait for the winter freeze. He divided his 6,500 man army into three columns. One, which was made up of Kentuckians, was sent to Fort Defiance in two feet of snow. The troops were reduced to living in squalor, the worst of all conditions of the Western army. When word reached Frankfort, Shelby went to the women of the state with a challenge to produce warm clothing which they did in great numbers. However, most of it was lost in transport, or delayed, due to the difficulties of transportation.

By mid-December Harrison readied his men for the attack on Detroit and on January 17 it was captured with ease. In response to a plea for help he also sent a large contingent to Frenchtown that was garrisoned with about 400 Canadian militia. It too was easily taken.

Harrison, for some unknown reason, elected to hold Frenchtown and awaited reinforcements from Detroit. Only eighteen miles away were great numbers of Indians and British soldiers at Malden.

When word reached Kentucky the entire state rejoiced. The good news was received by all since almost all families had a relative or friend in the army. Isaac's wife had a cousin with the victors. The jubilation did not last long. During a grand celebration at a Frankfort theater, which the governor and his wife attended, the evening came to an abrupt, early ending. A mud-spattered courier ran down the aisle to Shelby and whispered in his ear. He arose immediately and left the theater, that was suddenly erupting in the horrible speculation of some tragedy.

Hearing of the fall of Frenchtown, the British army in Canada made a forced march toward the River Raisin. Harrison's decision to hold the town can be called into question for its lack of poor posting and exposed lines and he paid for his blunder dearly. At dawn on the morning of January 22,

Chapter Eleven

more than 500 British regulars supported by more than 800 Indians chopped Harrison's army to pieces. More than 100 Kentuckians were scalped in the opening minutes and many others were shot down. Most of the force was captured with no more than thirty escapees. The ambulatory men were force-marched across the frozen Detroit River, while the seriously wounded, numbering between thirty and fifty, were left to the care of American surgeons. That night, the Indians returned and scalped many of the helpless men. One building was set on fire. The Indians waited outside the doors and windows with tomahawks and knives in hand and scalped and battered the screaming men as they fled the fire, some with their clothes blazing. The dead Kentuckians' bodies were left where they fell to be eaten by hogs and dogs, while the British officers did very little to prevent the butchery. In the eyes of the Kentuckians at home, British General William Proctor became a much hated man. The few that escaped reported that he had not only sanctioned the bloodletting but encouraged it by turning the prisoners over to the Indians.

Kentuckians by the hundreds rushed to sign up for a pursuit of the evil Proctor. Banners and broadsides carried the war cry to every village to "Remember the River Raisin!"

Immediately the Kentucky legislature voted to go into extended session and to provide more men for Harrison's relief. Shelby was then favored with a resolution asking his leadership whenever he felt it necessary to promote the public interest.

Harrison's winter campaign was stopped cold with the massacre of a large part of his forces. He marched his remaining exhausted and freezing men, about 1,000 in all, back to Fort Meigs. He was also losing many of his soldiers whose terms of enlistments were up.

From here he wrote an urgent letter to Governor Shelby for help. In March, Shelby replied that another 1,200 men were on their way. At the same time he wrote to federal government officials pointing out the disproportionate number of Kentuckians who were carrying the fighting responsibilities. He also insisted that the United States must take possession of the Great Lakes and he begged that the men be paid promptly. He also begged for more men, and a strong show of force instead of a half-hearted effort.

About this time Master Commandant Oliver H. Perry arrived on Lake Erie with his thirteen-year-old brother to supervise construction of a fleet of thirteen ships which he was to command.

About midnight on May 4, the 1,200-man relief force arrived in the vicinity of Fort Meigs commanded by General Green Clay, and accompanied by twenty-eight-year-old Major James Shelby, Isaac's oldest son. The fort had been under bombardment for four days and was hard-pressed. Harrison sent a messenger to the Kentuckians to destroy the British cannon. Clay assigned the job to Lt. Col. William Dudley's regiment to which James was attached. Clay divided his men into three columns with James

Answering the Call as the Bloodletting Begins 77

Shelby at the head of one. Shelby was directed to lead his men past the guns, then attack from the side while the remaining two columns would attack from the rear. Young Shelby, acting as his famous father might have, did not wait for the others to get into position. He lead a rapid charge of his men directly at the guns, screaming and shouting as they went, capturing the cannon without losing a single man.

The major's men jumped and shouted for joy at their complete victory and began a celebration on the enemy shoreline. On the opposite shore General Harrison began yelling for young Shelby to retreat as fast as possible. However, it is not known if Harrison's pleas were heard and ignored, or just ignored altogether. At the same time Harrison was failing to make his order heard, Shelby's men uncovered a small number of Indians in ambush, flushed them out, and began pursuit. This gave the British time to reorganize. As more Indians filled out the ranks, the order was given to attack the Kentuckians.

In the assault that followed the Kentuckians suffered another ignominious defeat. Of the 800 engaged, 600 or more were either killed or captured. The prisoners were marched to a British camp and herded into a small, compact circle. There the Indians began to randomly fire into the group of screaming and cursing men begging for their lives. Some were pulled from the circle and bludgeoned with tomahawks. Others were set on fire. This continued under the indifferent eyes of the British officers until the arrival of Tecumseh who placed himself between his men and the Kentuckians. Over the heated objections of many of his warriors, the slaughter was stopped. Storming to the tent of General Proctor he is alleged to have said, "You are not fit to command, go and put on your petticoats."

It was a week before the grievous news reached Kentucky. Among the dead was Major James Shelby. Isaac hung his head in grief. For the second time he had sent his fellow Kentuckians out to do battle and for the second time they had been massacred. Again, he reflected on how the federal government had been lax in fighting the war, and their polite rebuff of his advice. He understood that superior numbers were needed to accomplish the mission and there were not enough men at Fort Meigs to do the job right. Two battles had begun to deplete Kentucky's available manpower and he blamed Harrison for the losses. A few days later when Harrison arrived he placed the fault on the shoulders of Lieutenant Colonel Dudley's errors for the disaster and Isaac was quick to accept. And to the great relief of all, some of those, who were first reported killed, arrived at home. Among this group was Major James Shelby who received a tearful, joyous reception from his father and family. He had been captured and later exchanged by the British. He was promoted to the rank of major general of the 5th Division of Kentucky Militia and later, after the conflict ended, received the rank of brigadier general.

Chapter Eleven

Isaac rejoiced in the return of his son but found it necessary to face the on-going problem confronting Harrison. The general was now in receipt of a letter from the secretary of war granting Harrison permission to call up men from the neighboring states in such numbers as was needed for the Canadian expedition. He immediately sent a letter to Isaac with the information and asked for another two thousand men, and asking that the governor come in person to lead a command. Harrison said that although he would have much confidence in Isaac's leadership, that he, Isaac, would be the guiding head and he, Harrison, the guiding hand.

The reply from Frankfort was immediate. Governor Isaac Shelby, at age sixty-two, said that it would be his honor to fight under Harrison's banner. The call went out for volunteers to "avenge the blood of their butchered friends!" The appointed day for the men to join was August 31 and the location was Newport. "Kentucky volunteers," his call said, "I will meet you there in person and I will lead you to the field of battle and share with you the dangers and honors of the campaign!"

Chapter Twelve

☆☆☆☆☆☆☆☆☆☆☆☆☆☆☆

Shelby's Comin' Through!
Adventure in Canada

As the word spread around the state that "Old King's Mountain" was going to lead his Kentuckians again, state volunteers heartened to the anticipated leadership he would provide. Their old comrade-in-arms was in the saddle again and spoiling for a fight.

"Shelby's coming through," was the cry! Now a general, the tough, old Indian fighter would inspire his followers. For many of the Ohioans it was the first time they had seen him in over ten years.

On the last day of August, Kentuckians answered Shelby's call to arms to the number of 3,500 mounted men. Among them was another famous frontiersman, explorer and Indian fighter named Simon Kenton. The two shared a joyous reunion. Simon would, at Isaac's request, join the expedition as a respected counselor. Kenton was now fifty-eight years old and tired from his many years on the trail, running many Indian gauntlets and hand-to-hand combat. His family protested loudly, citing his age, bad legs, and general physical condition. With his head bowed he nodded in agreement giving the impression that he would not join the expedition, to the great relief of his family. Later, when the company rode out of Urbana to the north it was without Kenton. Several hours later he saddled up his horse and rode casually away as if to go home. A few miles out of town he contacted a friend and asked him to deliver to his family a message that he was on his way to join Shelby. There was an ulterior motive to Kenton's actions. Unknown to his family, a soldier who had been with his son had told him that his son, Simon Kenton, Jr., was a prisoner of the Indians. Simon planned to find out for himself.

A grand review was conducted by Isaac who was mounted with a handsome sword hanging by his side. This was the sword voted for him by the North Carolina legislature in grateful recognition of his leadership at King's Mountain, thirty years past. The legislature, for some reason, never made the award; rather, Isaac had to ask for it.

Chapter Twelve

Prior to the assembly, Shelby had made numerous inquiries and plans for supplies. The army would be short 700 rifles but he would not wait on the government for them, since it seemed indifferent to the cause most of the time. He would collect arms along the line of march to avoid any further delays. Among his plans were the placing of surgeons and medical supplies at Detroit to be available when the fighting began. When one of the surgeons suggested that the hospitals and stores accompany the troops Isaac lost his temper. He shouted at the surgeon, "Do you think sir, that I am leading an expedition of sick men? You shant have a single wagon, sir: I whipped Ferguson without one and can do the same for Proctor!"

The expedition crossed the Ohio River for the march of two weeks to Michigan. It was after the troops had left the state that the federal government approved Isaac's call for mounted men who then arrived many days later in Frankfort.

Isaac led his men into Upper Sandusky and learned that a great Wyandot chief had heard of his coming and waited to meet "the famous Shelby." After the meeting the small army moved to General Harrison's camp at Lower Sandusky. On arrival the men cheered the news that on September 10 Commodore Perry had engaged the British fleet in an extended gun battle between nine American ships and six British. At the conclusion of the day's engagement Perry sent a hastily written note to General Harrison reading, "We have met the enemy and they are ours!"

On the arrival of Shelby's men at Lower Sandusky he learned that Perry was also there, having come by ship with many British prisoners. The victorious commodore, amid gleeful congratulations from Shelby and Harrison, volunteered to act as an aide in the coming battle. Perry was acknowledged for having broken the British control of the Great Lakes and opening the route to Upper Canada. Isaac was now almost singlehandedly responsible for 4,500 men poised on the shores of Lake Erie. There were enough men to do the job and the time was right. (Perry, who was the exact same age as Isaac's oldest son, gave him a souvenir of the famous battle on Lake Erie: a marine telescope taken from the British ship *Queen Charlotte*.)

The entire army was in camp in the following two days and the one thousand men, commanded by Colonel Richard M. Johnson, began the overland march to Detroit. A long fence was constructed between the Portage River and the bay to confine the horses. One problem arose. It required a draft of men who would remain behind to care for their mounts. Not a single man wanted to waste the long miles they had marched to stay behind and watch the horses. Yet, it wasn't an easy job. On one occasion thousands of horses stampeded killing several men.

Harrison's plan was a basic one. Johnson and his men were to march around the tip of Lake Erie toward Detroit while Harrison's infantry was ferried in transports by Perry's fleet to a point near Fort Malden

Shelby's Coming Through! Adventure in Canada   81

(Amherstburg). The two forces would then converge on the fort from opposite directions and smash the enemy.

With the United States in complete control of Lake Erie at this time Proctor knew he could not defend both Amherstburg and Detroit simultaneously. He reluctantly elected to burn down the fort's stockades and retreat eastward toward the Niagara frontier.

As nearly nine-hundred mounted redcoats and fifteen hundred Indians rode away from the burning fort a column of black smoke swirled upward toward the sky. Riding to the high ground above the fort, Tecumseh turned his horse around and studied the scene before him. To his chief aide, Chau-be-nee, the Coalburner, and to his brother-in-law, Wasegoboah, he said, "My Brothers, I feel well assured that we will never return again." Astride their mounts they looked at one another for a moment then turned to study the enlarging columns of smoke as if looking for a sign that their leader's words were not true.

Tecumseh's dream of a great Indian confederacy was about to collapse. And it would not end in a great battle, but in a cowardly retreat. He demanded a meeting with Proctor. The two warriors met on September 18, in a storagehouse at Amherstburg. General Proctor had been stunned at news of Perry's victory and the opening of a path for the Americans into Canada. Again Tecumseh came down hard on the British officer. The Indian chief's scouts told a different story of Perry's fight as he screamed opposition to Proctor's plans. He compared Proctor to a fat dog running away with its tail between its legs. Proctor's face became blood red at the blistering verbal assault by the Indian chief and at the end of his harangue his braves leaped to their feet, waving knives and tomahawks in a threatening manner. Proctor, perhaps apprehensive for his and his men's lives, reconsidered. We will not retreat to the Niagara frontier he blurted, rather, we will make a stand at Delaware Moravian Indian Town on the Thames River. There, he said, we will defeat Harrison, or "lay our bones! Tecumseh was relieved. Now, he thought, at least he had been successful in getting Proctor to make a stand.

On September 20, the army reached Put-in-Bay, where Perry had won his victory, then pushed on to one of the sister islands, covered with slime and about six acres in size. Before camp could be set up the men had to scrape the ground of snail fluids, making living conditions despicable. As more soldiers arrived, living space vanished. To rest became impossible. Mildew and the overall filth of the land produced some sickness. The lack of much good food led to some illnesses that were serious enough to force leaving some men behind as the march continued. They had only rotten meat to eat.

Harrison prepared on the theory that the battle would begin immediately as the first boats set his men on Canadian soil in front of Fort

Chapter Twelve

Malden. The left wing was assigned to Shelby's men. Harrison believed they would take the brunt of the attack carried out by the Indians.

Boats were loaded on Monday, September 27, 1813. As the work began, the winds increased in force making conditions miserable and the boats hard to handle. At one point the blasting winds blew ashore the body of a sailor who had been killed in Perry's battle and who was still tied to a 32-pound cannonball. To get to the boats for loading, the men had to wade in the frigid waters up to their crotches. They were soaked and hungry and most of their clothing was frozen to their bodies. Nevertheless, memories of their fallen comrades instilled a spark in their souls to meet and defeat the enemy. Shelby is reported to have drawn his sword and taken a position on the ship's bow, pointing the weapon toward the Canadian shore. He would later say that the crossing to Canada, on the biggest body of water that he or any other Kentuckian had ever seen, was truly an act of God.

Late in the afternoon the army went ashore on the other side of the lake and marched forward singing "Yankee Doodle" at the top of their lungs. But the only humans they discovered were the cowering citizens of the small town of Amherstburg, fearing the "barbarians" as described to them by the British.

Four miles from Amherstburg, Fort Malden was smoldering and in ruins. The British burned it as they evacuated in haste before a rumored vast army of Kentuckians seeking vengeance for the River Raisin massacre. Proctor was fearful of the avenging Americans and at the same time had reservations about the reliability of his Indian allies. His position was untenable and Tecumseh knew it. Considering the alternatives and the help available, Proctor reasoned that his decision to retreat no farther than the Thames River was sound. And despite being constantly berated by Tecumseh, and accused of cowardice, Proctor continued his retreat for the better part of seven days.

By the end of September Johnson and Harrison's forces were joined. The two pressed their men hard in pursuit of the enemy.

The army was only five miles along the path of the retreating British and Indians when a party of sixty Wyandots led by Chief Walk-in-Water, who was carrying a flag of truce, emerged from the woods. The chief explained that his people were rejecting the British, refused to fight, and wanted to live in peace with the white man. Harrison told him that it was good what they had done and that all they had to do was to go home and stay out of the way of the American army. Having expected terms much more severe the chief turned his men around at once and rode off.

Proctor eventually was compelled to turn and fight for fear of having his slow-moving rear guard overrun by the hard-riding Americans. Colonel Richard M. Johnson's 1,000-man cavalry unit led the way followed by Shelby and his Kentuckians. Johnson's cavalry did not carry

Shelby's Coming Through! Adventure in Canada   83

the traditional sabers. Instead, they were armed with rifles, pistols, tomahawks, and long knives.

They covered twenty-five miles the first day. At the fort, one horse had been found that the British had not taken with them. This was given to Shelby whose legs were causing him some discomfort. He reminded his men that to defeat the enemy, one must do more than he does by early and forced marches. The men accepted the challenge in good spirits. As the line neared the mouth of the Thames a hovering eagle was spotted and all agreed that it was a symbol of a future success. Perry recalled that on the day he defeated the British fleet on Lake Erie, he too had seen an eagle soaring high above the waters.

The rapidly retreating British dropped many supplies, including food, clothing, and powder as they raced away from the lake. The Americans scavenged what they could use and were also successful in capturing a small band of Indians and a small British boat loaded with ammunition.

Tecumseh, eager to get the fight started, kept prodding Proctor to turn and fight. Only to have the officer say he wanted to move along a little farther. At one point Tecumseh stayed at one location and took on the rapidly advancing Americans. In minutes Johnson's men attacked the Indian chief's small party. The Indians broke off contact once Johnson brought up several pieces of artillery. There were few casualties on both sides; however, Tecumseh did suffer a slight arm wound.

The morale among the British was extremely poor. Proctor's ranks had been greatly diminished by a high number of recent desertions and attrition. He could count on about 600 regular troops and about 1,500 Indians. The soldiers feared the wrath of the Americans whom they knew would be seeking a bloody revenge on them. Many wrote their last letters to families at home in anticipation of the worst.

Proctor was perhaps not the most formidable of British soldiers, but to his credit he did have a good eye for defensive positions. Reigning in his army, he positioned them in a superb defensive line about two miles west of the Moraviantown. On his left was the Thames River with a very steep bank acting as a natural barrier to any flanking attack. On his right was a swamp that paralleled the river for several miles, which also provided a natural barrier to flanking operations by the enemy. The ground between the river and swamp was covered with a very thick growth of beech, maple and oak trees, but not very much underbrush.

Harrison's scouts found the British in a somewhat unusual, skirmishing line. There were two loose lines, one that ran along the river in a stand of beech trees, and a second that stretched between the river and a swamp. The Indians, apparently, were concealed in the area between the two swamps.

Proctor had positioned Tecumseh and the main body of some 1,500 Indians in the swamp, thinking that they should be able to outflank the

84   Chapter Twelve

Americans from there. The British regulars and several hundred Canadian militia formed two parallel lines facing the advancing Americans between the swamp and the river. They were ready for a fight, but not comfortable with the anticipated outcome.

About fifteen miles away Harrison and Shelby sat around a campfire discussing their options. The men were urged to "remember the massacre at the Raisin River."

Shelby's men were placed in position to charge the British regulars. During the night he walked among his men, talking with them and making last minute preparations. At dawn the army moved out on the road to Moraviantown and as scouts returned to the two commanders, Shelby began to get a visual image of what was ahead, and issued orders for the final disposition of his men. Meanwhile, Harrison had studied the reports of his scouts and quickly changed his plan of attack based on this information. He sent orders to Shelby to move to a strategic point on the right that would allow his mounted warriors to gallop quickly to any part of the battlefield where they would be needed. Johnson's men would attack through the narrow opening leading to Proctor's battleline. Colonel Johnson realized at once that the narrow passage was too small for all of his men to pass through safely, so he divided the battalion. His brother took half with him to charge the British regulars while Johnson took the other 500 to cross the swamp toward the Indians. Harrison's decision to use mounted infantry to lead the attack was, at the time, considered "unusual," or, at least, "somewhat daring!" He admitted afterwards that he had no military precedent for the attack design, but admitted that the American backwoodsmen did ride better in the woods than any other people. He was also convinced that the retreating enemy would be surprised, indeed at the first attack wave and unprepared to face his men. And he was right. For the battle on that day of October 5, 1813 would last well beyond an hour, but it would be settled in the first five minutes.

Chapter Thirteen

☆☆☆☆☆☆☆☆☆☆☆☆☆☆☆

Remembering the River Raisin

The Battle of the Raisin River was vivid in the minds of these men who were anxious for revenge. They learned of the British officers who deliberately overlooked the scalping of a number of Kentuckians who had been taken prisoner. As the moment of battle neared, each man conjured up images of what it must have been like to have been there. The screaming of these men for mercy was heard as the Indians passed among them swinging their tomahawks in giant arcs that came smashing downward on the skulls of their comrades and the severing of the scalp from the head. These gruesome images hardened the men to the task ahead.

At last the moment arrived. The bugles blasted the charge that carried over the battlefield and enveloped Johnson's men like a shroud as they advanced on the British, shouting at the top of their lungs, "Remember the River Raisin!" Johnson's first charge scattered the British line, sending Proctor's men running pell-mell in all directions. As the cavalry poured into the lines slashing away and firing on the gallop, some ran into heavy stands of trees and dismounted. Feeling the momentum would not be stopped, they pushed on toward the second British line about thirty yards to the rear of the first line. It too was quickly smashed. As fast as the British could throw down their arms they raised their hands in surrender to the delight of the victors. Harrison reported that one officer and about fifty men escaped. The gunfire gradually ceased as the battlefield fell silent.

With that portion of the field under control Johnson turned his men toward the swamp where his scouts had indicated the Indians might be in position, however, he was unable to detect their presence. The only way to break the silence, he reasoned, was to draw their fire.

In the swamp Tecumseh watched as the British were scattered with ease by the Americans. Earlier, he had confided in his closest warrior leaders that he had dreamed that he would die in this day's fighting. He watched in great anxiety as Johnson's men easily crushed Proctor's two lines. It was time now to go forward and fight.

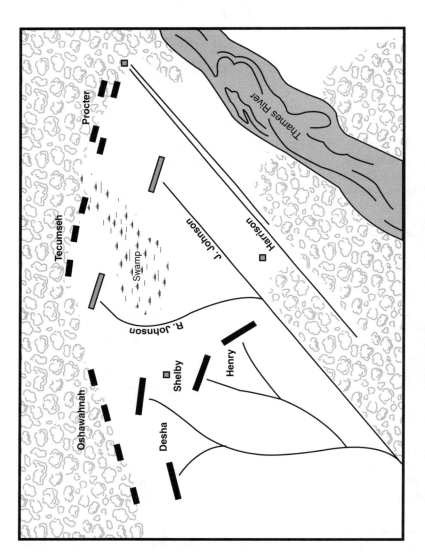

Map of the Battle of the Thames

Isaac Shelby, Kentucky's First Governor

Johnson surveyed the swamp and saw nothing. Then, he called forward nineteen volunteers to ride with him into the swamp. Afterwards this group would be referred to by many as "The Forlorn Hope."

Into the swamp they rode, still unable to see the enemy. Then suddenly the grasses exploded with gunfire as the Indians sprang to their feet with their shrill war cries. More than one-half of the twenty were killed instantly.

Tecumseh raised himself out of the tall grass, leveled his rifle at Johnson, and fired. His first shot seriously wounded the cavalry commander but he remained on his mount though in great pain. Seeing the American leader wounded, the Indians instantly charged forward and into the face of the remainder of Johnson's battalion who came galloping onto the field. The undergrowth in the swamp was exceptionally thick in some places demanding some of the cavalry to dismount and engage in hand-to-hand battle.

At this moment Tecumseh and Johnson were face-to-face and only yards apart. Johnson pulled his pistol, pointed it at the veteran Indian leader, and fired. The bullet struck the great warrior flush in the face killing him instantly. As he fell the remainder of his braves stopped fighting and ran from the field. Many, believing that he was impervious to bullets, surrendered to the jubilant Americans.

In moments the Battle of the Thames was over. The Indians who did not surrender deserted the field leaving the British to be greatly despondent at their defeat. However, Proctor managed to escape much to the consternation of Harrison. Proctor had left the engagement in his carriage as the action began. He was later court-martialed and found guilty of misconduct.

When the Americans learned that the dreaded Tecumseh was dead, many began to search the battlefield for his body even though they had no idea what he looked like. One Kentuckian who did know him was Simon Kenton. A runner was sent to bring him to the grounds. As this was being done a number of Kentuckians began whetting their knives to get a "souvenir" of the great warrior.

Tecumseh
Courtesy Kentucky Historical Society

Chapter Thirteen

With Kenton's arrival the search of about three hundred dead Indians began. Most had to be turned over for identification and the process was lengthy. Finally, Kenton's face lit up. It was the chief, still in death, with a grim expression on his face that was covered with blood from the wound inflicted by the American. "Is that him, Simon?" the men asked.

"Yes," he said, "it is Tecumseh."

"By God," one soldier cried, "we got the devil himself."

American losses were about 15 killed and thirty wounded. British losses were 18 killed, 26 wounded, and more than 600 captured. Thirty-three bodies were found on the field the next day, but many had been removed including that of Tecumseh. To this day it is not known where he was buried by his warriors.

William Henry Harrison

War of 1812

For the next two days the Americans remained at the scene burying the dead. The Americans in one trench and the British in another. Harrison also sent a squad to burn nearby Moraviantown to deny its reoccupation.

Shelby took charge of the prisoners, including some women, and stragglers, and began the march back to American soil. He had participated in the most successful land battle of the war and helped bring to an end the Indian resistance in the Northwest. The outcome exonerated him of his prior convictions on strategy and strength in battle. This he would later point out to the secretary of war was also the least expensive campaign.

There were questions afterwards as to whether Johnson actually killed Tecumseh, a question he never answered. However, the celebrity he gained from the event propelled him to the vice-presidency of the United States under President Martin Van Buren, from 1837 to 1841.

The return march by the victorious army was anything but joyful. Shelby led his men to the lake but refused a boat ride with the sick and the wounded, electing instead to remain with his men. A choice the men happily sanctioned. On the march to Canada the morale was high and the objective drove each man to achieve a great victory. This they had accomplished.

Now most of the men were sick and exhausted. Their route took them over deep creeks covered with sharp edges of dangerous ice. Then there were swamps and thickets that dampened and tore open their clothing. Under these conditions progress was slow—twenty to twenty-five miles per day on half-empty stomachs. Half-rations of beef without bread or

Remembering the River Raisin

89

salt was all they had. Men began to give out and fall along the path near the end of each day's march. And to add to the confusion many men could not find their assigned companies and spent much energy making inquiries of men they did not know.

On arrival at Sandwich, the elements turned against them. Snow, sleet, freezing rain, and high winds battered and numbed the Patriots to the bone. Isaac turned over his prisoners, then he directed his men to Frenchtown on the Raisin River. On arrival the men marveled at the lushness of the orchards of food before them. They were immediately sickened on discovery of a great number of skulls and bones, unburied from the earlier massacre of their fellow Kentuckians. A full Christian burial was given to sixty-five skeletons.

Next, they arrived at Portage where their horses had been quartered. Most often horses were broken, many dead, and those that survived were on the verge of starvation. Shelby borrowed a horse from Harrison and continued to push his men at a rate of twenty-five miles a day. The return trip, most agreed, was worse than the battle. A steady rain lasted several days. The army had few tents and even fewer blankets. Men were soaked to the skin, but they continued on. Many went twenty-four hours at a time without food. Many died and were buried along the road in hastily dug graves.

The army was out of bread and salt. The small supply of beef was fought over by officers and enlisted men at times. Tempers flared and feelings were crushed.

Finally, in November, the army staggered across the Ohio River at Maysville (Limestone, Ky.), and was discharged at Newport on November 4.

Isaac Shelby made a farewell address to the survivors urging each to put behind him the "unpleasant sensations of the journey home." He urged that each man "return home united as a band of brothers with the sweet solace of having served our Country from the purest motives and to the best of our abilities."

The army was received with great joy and acclamation for their victory at the Thames. Coupled with Perry's victory on Lake Erie, America now held undisputed dominance in the Northwest.

Shelby received a great deal of praise, both local and national, for his service. While healing from the deprivations of the battle and the march to and from the scene, the governor of Kentucky realized that he had three more years to serve.

In June 1814, President Madison wrote a letter asking him to serve on a treatying commission to the defeated Northwest Indians. Shelby was concerned that should he accept the federal appointment would he be required to vacate the governor's office. He turned to a judge friend who ruled that the Constitution of the United States dictated that he could not hold both positions simultaneously. Reluctantly, he remained in Frankfort.

Chapter Thirteen

Harrison, in the meantime, had made some enemies in the political world. When Congress voted medals to Shelby and Harrison for their service in Canada, Harrison's enemies made a strong effort to have his name deleted from the resolution. Always loyal to his friends and comrades-in-arms, Shelby wrote Congressman Henry Clay of his embarrassment and anger because Harrison had "rendered ten times more service to the nation than I had." Harrison's name remained and it wasn't until 1818 that Congress finally cleared the awards. And it was months later that Isaac had to ask for his.

In 1815 the British tired of long inactivity in the North and massed their troops for an attack on New Orleans. Washington sent Andrew Jackson to organize its defense. Shelby was once again called upon to provide men for the defense of his beloved country. Though at times he became irritated at the lack of support shown by other states; nevertheless, he called for 10,000 volunteers. Writing the War Department he said, "There is a great deal of patriotism in Kentucky, but we have not the arms or ammunition to fight the country's battles." Still, the War Department sent no supplies. Isaac's own quartermaster risked his own fortune by borrowing money to supply the troops and to send them by boat to Jackson. In the end, only 2,200 men were deemed fit to fight and most made the trip without guns and ammunition, much to the consternation of Jackson. "I have never seen a Kentuckian without a gun and a pack of cards and a bottle of whiskey in my life!" he exclaimed.

These Kentuckians were not violent men that the citizens of New Orleans were accustomed to seeing on the Mississippi, cursing, drunk and always in a fight. Rather, they were quieter. Still, those who came to New Orleans unarmed did what they considered proper when the British attacked. They ran away! Jackson, on January 8, 1816, threw a mighty British invasion force back into the Gulf of Mexico with practically no casualties of his own. The overwhelming victory at the mouth of the mighty Mississippi was somewhat overshadowed by the eventual knowledge that the war had been over for two weeks.

Chapter Fourteen

☆☆☆☆☆☆☆☆☆☆☆☆☆☆☆
The Traveler Rests

With the war's end Shelby feared that negotiations would give away the territory that he and Harrison had captured from the British. The British eventually gave up their demands for a large buffer state for the Indians and the Americans gave up their initial request for Canada.

Isaac, satisfied with the terms, settled in at Traveler's Rest. Among the many bills that came out of his second administration was one that put convicts to work making nails.

His second daughter, Letitia, was married in January 1816 to a young lawyer who had served at the Thames, Charles Stewart Watson. A consummate politician, he would later serve as secretary of state to President Madison and after that in the House of Representatives. Isaac, always kind to his children, built the couple a home five miles north of Shelbyville, modeled after the elaborate governor's mansion in Frankfort.

As his term of office neared its end his friends began working on his behalf as a candidate for vice president. He wrote letters to the local papers insisting that he did not want to seek the high office. He was tired and wanted to go home, and stay. In 1837 his good friend, Harrison, won the office. His fame was due almost solely to the fact that he was "the person who killed Tecumseh." Andrew Jackson, the hero of New Orleans, defeated Henry Clay for the presidency and became the nation's seventh president.

His second term ended in September 1816. As he left office a national salute was fired with the cannon taken from the British at Saratoga, given up to them at Detroit and then reclaimed at the Thames. The cannon was later presented by the government to Shelby. Free at last, he went home, sat down at his desk, and wrote: "1816, Friday evening 6th September I returned home from Frankfort having served as governor for four years and ten days from the 25th of August 1812 on which day I was sworn into office, to this the 4th day of September 1816...on which day at night I went out of the office and left the seat of government the next day."

Chapter Fourteen

Within the week he was totally absorbed in his farm work and a happy, satisfied man. His family felt the pangs of the war in many ways. His daughter Susan Hart was now a widow, her husband James McDowell died in 1812, a very short time after being named a lieutenant in the Kentucky militia. His daughter Nancy died in 1815. Weeks later eighteen-year-old-son James died, and shortly thereafter Isaac's half-brother James, the younger son of his father's second marriage, died when he fell from a horse. And Letitia, his half-sister by that marriage, also died in western Kentucky.

Ill health was now the constant companion of Isaac and Susannah. Both required periods of rest but were unable to get caught up with many family obligations demanding their time and decreasing energies.

As the years passed and grandchildren arrived through on-going marriages, all of his children named a child after their famous grandfather. Isaac and Susannah's offspring produced more than sixty grandchildren.

On many occasions the men who had served with him in all of his battles for freedom would stop by for a visit to recall their times together. Any who were down on their luck would quickly be accommodated. Those who needed help of any kind received it. Isaac remained active in all aspects of his later years. He was a founder of the Kentucky Bible Society in 1813 and in 1816 he became vice president of the new American Bible Society. He was named president of the board of trustees for Centre College, in Danville, when it was chartered in 1819. Isaac remained active throughout his life in one of his favorite organizations, the Kentucky Society for Promoting Useful Arts.

In 1817 Isaac turned down a request from his personal friend President James Monroe to be named secretary of war. Isaac recommended William Henry Harrison.

Nevertheless, Isaac was one of the singularly qualified Americans to talk treaty with the Chickasaw Indians for the only large Indian claim left on the western land between the Tennessee and Mississippi Rivers. For many years he had urged the federal government to purchase the valuable land from the Indians. In June 1818, President Monroe named Isaac and Andrew Jackson to a commission to make the purchase. Friendship and respect between him and the Indians had remained over the years. On many occasions the Indians on their way to trade used Traveler's Rest as a stopping place—a place where they were supplied with all of their needs and enjoyed many long hours swapping tales with "Old King Shelby."

The trip began in September of 1818 toward Tennessee. It was not comfortable for Isaac whose legs gave him great pain at times. Occasionally he would have to dismount to allow circulation to normalize. He was able to rest for a while at the home of Andrew Jackson, but as always, when word spread of his presence in the neighborhood, citizens always wanted to meet and honor him with gifts and great displays of food and affection.

The Traveler Rests 93

The party finally arrived in Old Town and began negotiations with the Chickasaw Nation. Their initial offer was an annuity of $20,000 per year for twelve years. That was rejected. The terms were extended to thirteen and then fourteen years. The Indians then asked for one cent more. The settlement had been reached, but when the time arrived to sit down and sign the agreement, the Indians made additional demands. This time for another year or an additional $20,000 to be paid in fifteen years. Jackson relented after some arguing, but Isaac shook his head and said in a firm voice, NO! The two argued a bit and as the differences heated up, Isaac called for his horse. Isaac's son-in-law Thomas Hart, acting as his secretary, stepped in to calm the old warrior. Finally a compromise. Jackson and a friend agreed to sign a bond for an extra $20,000. If the government failed to pay when it was time, then the small section of land within the treaty territory would go to the signers of the bond who would pay for it. So, for $300,000 to be paid over fifteen years the U.S. government took possession of 4,600 square miles. It was referred to as the Jackson Purchase, but the new county around the new city of Memphis was named for Shelby.

Once their mission was completed, Isaac pressed his horse and company hard to return to Traveler's Rest. They covered forty-five miles a day, despite Isaac's continuing poor circulation. Hereafter, he would not journey far from the friendly confines of Traveler's Rest.

The next year, 1919, President Monroe and Andrew Jackson came to see him. The meeting of these three energetic and famous Americans was in Lexington. They exchanged old tales and enjoyed many laughs.

Isaac was now in his sixty-ninth year.

During the last week of February he suffered a stroke that paralyzed his right arm and crippled his legs. He was treated with mercury and gradually recovered. However, he failed to follow his doctor's advice to stay inside and rest. Isaac continued to be active and with the assistance of several beautiful silver-headed canes, hobbled around his spacious farm.

Henry Clay, the great orator from the "Bluegrass State," spoke before the state legislature at about this time. He said,

> If you want to find an example of order, of freedom from debt, of economy, of expenditure falling below, rather then exceeding income you will go to the well-regulated family of a farmer. You will go to the house of such a man as Isaac Shelby. You will not find him haunting taverns, engaged in broils, [or] prosecuting angry lawsuits.

To a point Clay was wrong with his lawsuit remark. Isaac, like his father, had a strict sense of justice and was unshakable in the face of challenge. He seldom lost in a court fight.

Clay continued, "...what the individual family of Isaac Shelby is, I wish to see the nation in the aggregate become."

Chapter Fourteen

After recovering from his stroke, Isaac's health fluctuated. Despite attempts by his friends and colleagues to become embroiled in politics, he remained close to his farm and family. At times he could be seen hobbling around its acres on a cane, with his arm in a sling, giving orders for the care of his land. He also set about preparing for his death by planning for the division of his land to his children and heirs.

Isaac willed Traveler's Rest and all of its furniture, trappings, and animals to his wife Susannah. At the time of her death it would pass to Alfred, who was now in charge of the farm's operations, including its slaves. However, Alfred would never claim the property for his own. On December 1, 1832, at the age of twenty-eight, he died in a hunting accident, only a few short months before his mother's death.

The conflict with William Campbell rose again, but Isaac declined to wage the war of argumentation. Thereafter, Isaac committed to paper his full recollection of the Battle of King's Mountain, including twenty affidavits from its veterans or their descendants in support of his position.

"Old King's Mountain" remained religious in his last years. He became a member of several Bible societies and was a faithful member of the Danville Presbyterian Church. Then, in 1816 he built a small, non-denominational church on his property. He also made final preparations for his burial in the family plot that already contained three of his children: Catherine, born in 1801 and who died in her infancy, and Nancy and John, along with other grandchildren who died from early childhood maladies.

On July 18, 1826, Isaac ate dinner with his family and went for a walk around the beautifully landscaped grounds of his beloved Traveler's Rest. Returning to the main building he spoke to his wife, sat down in a chair, sighed deeply, and died when a blood vessel broke in his head. He passed away without pain and suffering in his wife's arms.

His burial drew eulogies from a vast area. He was Kentucky's oldest hero, having arrived when it was only a wilderness filled with Indians and much danger. He was the first white man to set foot in many sections. His was the first Kentucky land settlement and pre-exemption granted by Virginia and at the time of his death, some forty-three years later, he was the last settler in the state still living on the original Virginia land grant of that period.

Isaac served as Kentucky's first governor and was instrumental in its gaining statehood, while fighting Indian wars. In 1812, at sixty-two, he was an aging elected governor who marched with his fellow Kentuckians to Canada to win back the Northwest from the British. He was referred to at his death as "The Father of Kentucky," in much the same manner as George Washington was for being the "Father of the United States." He was also called by many the "Father of the West."

Countless numbers of counties and towns, high schools and hospitals, along with many other institutions and structures, carry his name. In

This view of Traveler's Rest appeared on an old postcard.
Washington County Historical Society

1826, at his passing, the same month as the deaths of Thomas Jefferson and John Adams, many newspaper headlines mourned in heavy black print, *"Adams and Jefferson and Shelby are no more!"*

In 1827, the year after Isaac's death, the Commonwealth of Kentucky erected a monument in his honor, in the cemetery near Danville. On the south side it reads:

> Here rests the remains of ISAAC SHELBY Late Governor of Kentucky To whose memory The Legislature of the State Have erected this Monument.—Maryland gave him birth. He gave a life of Usefulness and Glory to the Nation.

On the east side:

> In the archives of his Country and the Pages of Faithful History His name will be presented to Posterity for the Administration and example of the PATRIOT, WARRIOR, STATESMAN AND PRIVATE CITIZEN. He was born Dec. 11, 1750 and on July 18th, 1836, Expired without a pang Full in the hopes of Immortality.

Isaac's burial place was accepted as a shrine in 1952 and restored. While all other Kentucky governors are buried in Frankfort, the Shelby family steadfastly refused to have him removed from his chosen site. He was laid to rest in the grounds that he loved most, and to which he had given so much of himself. The traveler was finally at rest.

Appendix A

Some of the Brave "Backwater Men" Who Served with Shelby at King's Mountain

(The names of many more men who fought at King's Mountain are known, but not the names of their commanding officers. Thus, the following list of Isaac's men is regrettably incomplete.)

ABERNATHY, ROBERT. Served as a delegate from Tyron County, North Carolina in 1776. Granted a pension by that state.

ADAIR, JOHN. Enter-taker for Sullivan County, North Carolina (now Tennessee.) Tax money was collected and turned over to Shelby and Sevier to finance the campaign against Ferguson.

ALLAN, MOSES. Was in several battles with the Indians and Tories before going to King's Mountain, under Shelby. Born in Baltimore, Maryland, he moved to Wilkes County, North Carolina, about 1770, and was in General Greene's army in 1781. Became a colonel in the militia, was elected first sheriff of Wilkes County and later was a member of the state legislature in 1793. Received a pension in Washington County, Virginia. Died at age ninety-one in Wilkes County in 1833.

ALLISON, JOHN. Wounded at King's Mountain. Suffered a knee injury that affected him the rest of his life. Supposed to have been a captain, as he was thereafter known as Captain John. His sons, Robert and David, were leading figures in attempts to form a separate state of Franklin, and active in Tennessee politics.

BEELER, JACOB. Survived the battle and took up residence in Sullivan County, North Carolina where he received a pension.

BEELER, JOSEPH. Brother to Jacob. Also settled in Sullivan County and was awarded a pension.

BELL, SAMUEL. A pioneer settler in Tennessee. His sword, used at King's Mountain, is in one of the rooms of the Tennessee Historical Society.

96

"Backwater Men" Who Served with Shelby 97

BELL, THOMAS. Brother to Samuel. Was twenty years old at the time of the battle. He had participated in many skirmishes before the battle. Received a pension in Montgomery County, Tennessee, in December 1833.

BLACKBURN, ROBERT. Also with Shelby in 1779 in the Chickamauga Campaign. His brother was reported to have been killed by a creek near Buchanan's Station, Davidson County, North Carolina by a party of roaming Indians. He was scalped and his body left with a spear sticking in it.

BRUSTER, E. No further record.

CARWELL, ALEXANDER. (1728–1803) A native of Ireland. Married Isabelle Brown.

CARWELL, JOHN. Son of Alexander. Married Sarah Wright. Received a bounty warrant for land located in Burke County, Georgia.

CHAMBERS, DANIEL. N/A

CHAMBERS, ROBERT. Believed to be related to Daniel.

CHANEY, THOMAS. N/A

CHRISTIAN, GILBERT. Born in Augusta County, Virginia, about 1734 and was an active participant in the Border Wars. Settled in the Holston country and commanded a company on Christian's Cherokee Campaign. Was prominent in organizing the Franklin Republic. A colonel in the Cherokee war of 1788. Died in Knoxville, Tennessee in 1793.

CLEMM, WILLIAM. Provided all needed equipment.

CLEVELAND, JOHN. The son of Colonel Cleveland was a captain of infantry at King's Mountain. Born in Virginia in 1760; died in Tugalo in 1812.

COBB, ARTHUR. Was active in assisting Shelby's troops. Born on the Watauga River.

COBB, PHAROH. Brother to Arthur. Served with Shelby at King's Mountain and Musgrove's Mill. His petition states that he saw service between 1776 and 1780, indicating that he was active in other fights.

COBB, WILLIAM, JR. Assisted Shelby's men on the way to King's Mountain with horses and supplies.

COBB, WILLIAM, SR. Along with his son, William, also aided Shelby. Was a justice of Washington County in 1778.

COCKE, WILLIAM. Native of Amelia County, Virginia, born in 1747. A captain under Shelby. As an elderly man he entered the service in the

98   **Appendix A**

war of 1812. Instrumental in forming the state of Franklin. Served in the legislatures of Virginia, North Carolina, Tennessee and Mississippi. Elected United States Senator from Tennessee. Died in Columbia, Mississippi, in 1828.

COLLINS, JAMES. Active in the fight and kept records for future generations.

COX, WILLIAM. Wounded in the fighting. Was a resident of the Watauga area in 1775. In 1793 he became a justice in the first court of Jefferson at the house of Jeremiah Williams.

CROCKETT, JOHN. The father of Davy Crockett was a participant with the militia from Lincoln County. He was born in Ireland or on the sea on the way across the Atlantic. He married Rebecca Hawkins of Maryland, who was related to the wife of Colonel Sevier. (Davy was born the fifth of nine children.) (Walter Crockett, John's brother, also fought at King's Mountain.)

CULBERTSON, JOSIAH. One of the best sharpshooters in Shelby's regiment. At King's Mountain and some men were ordered to gain an elevated position hotly contested by a Tory captain. In minutes Culbertson and his men killed the captain and drove his men off. He also played an important part in the fighting at Musgrove's Mill.

DAUGHERTY, GEORGE. A captain under Shelby and Sevier. Was active in 1778 in keeping the Cherokees from joining the British. Was active in formation of Franklin and Tennessee. A captain in the later campaigns against the Indians.

DAWSON, ELIAS. Fought with Shelby. No other record.

DELANEY, WILLIAM. Was an orderly sergeant under Shelby. One of the first settlers near Bristol, Tennessee.

DETGAOORETT, JOHN. Provided tomahawk and other weapons. Fought at Shelby's side in the border war battles (Virginia, North and South Carolina) in the early months of 1780. Is believed to have been with him at King's Mountain.

ELLIOT, JAMES. An early settler on the Holston. An ensign in 1777 and through good service rose to the rank of captain, commanding his own company at King's Mountain. Was killed in an ambush while serving under Colonel Arthur Campbell in the Cherokee expedition, at Tellico in December of 1780.

FAGAN, JOHN. Wounded at King's Mountain.

FAPOLSON, ANDREW. Served in Captain Evan Shelby's Company and participated in many border engagements.

"Backwater Men" Who Served with Shelby   **99**

FLEMING, JOHN. N/A.

FRIGGS, JOHN (OR FRIGGE). Served under Major Evan Shelby in Isaac Shelby's regiment.

FRIGGS, ROBERT. Also served under Major Evan Shelby in Isaac Shelby's regiment. Believed to have been a brother of John Friggs.

HARMISON, JOHN. N/A.

HARWOOD, WILLIAM. Provided all equipment including a tomahawk.

HENDRICKS, DAVID. Served with Shelby. His brother fought with Colonel Campbell.

HICKMAN, JAMES. A native of Virginia, where he served as a captain of militia. He served as a private under Shelby and was pensioned in Shelby County, in 1833, at the age of seventy-two.

HICKMAN, JOEL. Brother to James and also served under Shelby. Pensioned in Clay County, Kentucky, where he died in 1833.

HIGGINS, JOHN. N/A.

HUDSON, JOHN. Pensioned in Sullivan County, North Carolina in 1833 at age eighty-four.

HUFACRE, GEORGE. Often mentioned in the records of Washington County, Virginia. Pensioned in Knox County, North Carolina at age seventy-seven.

IRELAND, HANS. Very active in fighting at King's Mountain.

JACK, JAMES. A private under Isaac. Pensioned in Green County, Tennessee in 1833 at age seventy-seven.

JARNIGAN, THOMAS. Pensioned in Jefferson.

JARNIGAN, WILLIAM. Brother to Thomas. Also pensioned at Jefferson.

JENNINGS, DAVID. With Shelby but there is no record of being pensioned.

JOHNSON, BARNETT. Also served with Shelby in the Chickamauga Campaign of 1779.

Besides his service at King's Mountain, he was in action in the Snow Campaign, the siege of Fort Ninety-Six, and numerous engagements with the Cherokee Indians and the Tories. At King's Mountain he commanded a troop of ninety reserves who were called into action. He died in 1805.

JOHNSON, JAMES. Son of Henry Johnson, of Ireland. Born in Lincoln County in 1742. Served in the Snow Mountain Campaign, the siege

100   Appendix A

of Fort Ninety-Six, in various campaigns against the Cherokees and Tories and at King's Mountain. He captured a Tory officer (Patrick Moore) in hand-to-hand combat despite receiving a deep saber wound in the hand. This prevented him from firing his rifle when several British officers rushed him, allowing Moore to escape. At King's Mountain he commanded ninety reserves who were called into action under Shelby. He died in 1805. He had accumulated a vast estate on the Catawba River known as "Oak Grove." Prior to the war he had married Jane Ewart, the eldest daughter of Robert Ewart, of the North Carolina line. She died in 1795. They produced twelve children with several becoming distinguished citizens.

JUDD, JOHN. Moments before the Patriots took their positions around the base of King's Mountain, Shelby said that if anyone wanted to stay back that they must go at once. John Judd was the only man to respond and was given the job of holding the horses.

JUDD, ROWLAND. Brother to John, he was in the thickest of the fighting.

KARR (CARR), ROBERT. Lived in what is now Greene County, North Carolina. He fought at Point Pleasant under Evan Shelby and at King's Mountain under Isaac Shelby.

KEYS, JAMES. A lieutenant in Washington County, Virginia, he served under Shelby. Was pensioned in 1835.

KING, WILLIAM. Served under Shelby and pensioned in Sullivan County. His brother was under Campbell.

LANE, AQUILA. Born on 1755 and died in 1819. Married Agnes Fitzgerald, of Washington County, Tennessee, in 1780. Had seven children. Marched with Shelby's men to King's Mountain.

LANG, JOHN. Under Shelby, but nothing else is known.

LATMAN, JOSEPH. Under Shelby but nothing else is known.

LITTON, CATEL. One of Shelby's men. Other information not available.

LONG, JOHN. Settled in Sullivan County after the war.

LONG, WILLIAM. Was with Shelby, but no other information is available.

McADEN, WILLIAM. One of the earlier settlers along the Watauga.

McCLELLAND, JOHN. After King's Mountain he was sent to Westpoint Station to keep the Indians from molesting the Cumberland settlement.

McSPEDDEN, WILLIAM. He was with Isaac at King's Mountain and with Evan in the Chickamauga Campaign.

MANOR, THOMAS. One of Shelby's men but nothing else known.

"Backwater Men" Who Served with Shelby 101

MAXWELL, GEORGE. Born in Virginia in 1751, went early to the Holston. Became a lieutenant in 1777. Commanded a company under Isaac Shelby at King's Mountain. One of the first justices of Sullivan County, North Carolina, and held other important offices.

Active in early frontier service against the Indians. Member of the General Assembly of the short-lived Republic of Franklin. Died in 1822 at age seventy-two.

MAXWELL, THOMAS. Brother to George. Said the action at King's Mountain began at the east end of the mountain where Shelby and Campbell were opposed by Ferguson's forces.

MILLON, ———. In Evan Shelby's command at King's Mountain. Fought in the Chickamauga Campaign.

MORGAN, ISAAC. In the thick of the fighting.

MORGAN, THOMAS. Brother to Isaac. Along with Henry Reynolds discovered Warm Springs on the French River while on a scouting mission in 1778.

NELSON, WILLIAM. Served in Tipton's company of Shelby's regiment. Pensioned in Hawkins County, Tennessee in 1833 at age eighty-seven.

O'GULLION, BARNEY. Served with Shelby at King's Mountain and in the Chickamauga Campaign.

O'GULLION, HUGH. Brother to Barney. Also served at King's Mountain and in Chickamauga Campaign with Shelby.

PARKE, GEORGE. At King's Mountain and in the 1779 Chickamauga Campaign with Isaac.

PEMBERTON, CAPTAIN JOHN. In Shelby's regiment.

PENDEREGAST, GARRETT. Was in the fight with Shelby.

PERKINS, ELISHA. Another of Shelby's men.

PIERCE, JAMES. One of Isaac's expert riflemen. Also fought in the 1779 Chickamauga Campaign.

POLSON, ANDREW. Served in Captain Shelby's company at King's Mountain. Also fought in the Chickamauga Campaign.

PRATHER, CHARLES. With Shelby at King's Mountain and the Chickamauga Campaign.

PRICE, SAMUEL. Veteran of King's Mountain and Shelby's Chickamauga Campaign.

REESE, JAMES. Lived in Green County, North Carolina and voted in support of the state of Franklin.

Appendix A

ROBERTSON, MAJOR CHARLES. An early settler in northwest North Carolina.

His name often appeared on court records of 1777–1780. Fought with Isaac at Point Pleasant, Musgrove's Mill and was wounded at Cedar Springs.

RUTLEDGE, GEORGE. Born in Ireland in 1755 and died at Blountsville, Tennessee in 1813. Settled in Sullivan County in 1777 and joined with Shelby at King's Mountain. In 1774 he accompanied Daniel Boone to Powell's Valley. Between 1791 and 1794 he served with Wayne in their Indian campaigns. In 1808 he was in the regular army and commanded a company in the War of 1812. He died in 1825 at age sixty-six.

SAWYER, JOHN. Born in Virginia in 1745 shortly after his parents arrived from England, and were among the early settlers in Augusta County, Virginia. Active in frontier service against the Indians. Explored the Holston Valley. Served at Point Pleasant, on Major Gilbert Christian's Cherokee Campaign and the Chickamauga Campaign of 1779. Led a company at King's Mountain. Settled in Knox County, Tennessee. Twice elected to the state legislature. Died in 1831 at age eighty-six.

SNODGRASS, JAMES. Served with either Shelby or Campbell. Records are unclear.

WALLACE, THOMAS. Born in Maryland in 1745, and died in Montgomery County, Alabama, in 1830. Married Rebecca Milligan who lived until the age of ninety-one. They produced four children.

WEBB, DAVID. Brother to George. Served with Isaac.

WEBB, GEORGE. Landowner on the Watauga. Served on grand juries. One of first settlers in Greasy Cove. A company of Indians followed him there threatening to kill him unless he moved. Webb rounded up more settlers and was not bothered thereafter. Served as a captain under Shelby.

WELLS, JOSEPH. Served with Shelby at King's Mountain and in the Chickamauga Campaign.

The Roster of Captain Evan Shelby's Company of Volunteers from Fincastle County at the Battle of Point Pleasant

Capt. Evan Shelby: Capt. Isaac Shelby: Lt. James Robertson: Sgt. Valentine Sevier; Sgt. James Shelby; John Sayers; John Findley, Henry Shaw, Daniel Mungle, John Williams, John Carmack, Andrew Terrence, George Brooks, Isaac Newland, Abraham Newland, George Ruddle, Emanual Shoatt, Abram Bogard, Peter Torney, William Tucker, John Fain, Samuel Vance, Samuel Hensley, Samuel Samples (wounded), Conrad Nave, Arthur Blackburn, Robert Herrel, George Armstrong, William Casey, Mark Williams, John Stewart (wounded), Richard Burck, John Riley, Elijah Robinson, Rees Price, Richard Holliway, Jerrett Williams, Julias Robison, Charles Fiedler, Benjamin Grahum, Andrew Goff, Hugh O'Gullion, Barnett O'Gullion, Patrick St. Lawrence, Joseph Hughey (Killed), John Bradley and Basil Maxwell.

(The above list of Captain Evan Shelby's Volunteers from Fincastle County, Virginia is printed from an original in his own handwriting.)

Appendix B

Letter from Colonel Isaac Shelby to his Father, General Evan Shelby
[From the VIRGINIA GAZETTE, Nov. 4th, 1780]

I have herewith the pleasure to acquaint you, that on Saturday, the 7th instant., in the afternoon, we came upon Ferguson and his crew, who lay encamped on the top of King's Mountain. The day was wet, and the Providence who always rules and governs all things for the best, so ordered it that we were close around them before we were discovered, and formed in such position, so as to fire on them nearly about the same time, though they heard us in time to form, and stood ready. The battle continued warm for an hour, the enemy finding themselves so embarrassed on all sides, surrendered themselves prisoners to us at discretion.

They had taken post at that place with the confidence that no force could route them; the mountain was high, and exceedingly steep, so that the situation gave them greatly the advantage; indeed it was almost like storming a battery. In most places we could not see them until we were twenty yards of them. They repelled us three times with charged bayonets, but being determined to conquer or die, we came up a fourth time and fairly got possession of the top of the eminence. Our loss I have not exactly collected, as the camp has been in such disorder; but believe the killed to be about thirty-five men and between fifty and sixty wounded. (These are Patriot numbers.)

A list of killed, wounded, and prisoners of the British: Killed, Major Ferguson, one captain, two surgeons, and twenty-six privates. Wounded, one lieutenant and twenty-six privates. Prisoners, one captain, five lieutenants, one surgeon and fifty privates.

Tories killed: Two colonels, two captains, and one hundred and twenty-five privates. Wounded, one hundred and twenty-five. Prisoners, one colonel, one major, twelve captains, and eleven lieutenants, two ensigns, two adjutants, one commissary, one quartermaster, eighteen sergeants, and six hundred privates. Total, one thousand sixteen; seventeen baggage wagons and twelve stands of arms were taken.

Letter from Colonel Isaac Shelby to his Father 105

Our losses of killed and wounded: Colonel Williams, of South Carolina; Captain Edmondson, and five lieutenants from Virginia, and 23 privies from different states. Wounded, fifty-four from the different states.

Appendix C

The 1818 Treaty with the Chickasaw Indians

This treaty with the Chickasaws, to settle all territorial controversies, and to remove all grounds of complaint or dissatisfaction that might arise to interrupt the peace and harmony which have so long and so happily existed between the United States of America and the Chickasaw Nation of Indians, **JAMES MONROE,** President of the said United States, **ISAAC SHELBY** and **ANDREW JACKSON,** of the one part, and the whole Chickasaw Nation, by their chiefs, head men, and warriors, in full council assembled, of the other part, have agreed on the following articles, which when ratified by the President and the Senate of the United States of America, shall form, a treaty binding on all parties.

ARTICLE 1. Peace and friendship are hereby firmly established and made perpetual, between the United States of America and the Chickasaw Nation of Indians.

ARTICLE 2. To obtain the object of the foregoing article, the Chickasaw Nation of Indians cede to the United States of America (with the exception of such reservation as shall be hereafter mentioned) all claim or title which the said nation has to the land lying north of the south boundary of the state of Tennessee, which is bounded on the south by the thirty-fifth degree of north latitude, and which lands, hereby ceded, lies within the following boundary, viz.: Beginning on the Tennessee River, about thirty-five miles by water, below Colonel George Colbert's ferry, where the thirty-fifth degree of north latitude strikes the same, thence, due west, with said degree of north latitude, to where it cuts the Mississippi River at or near the Chickasaw Bluffs; thence, up the said Mississippi River, to the mouth of the Ohio; thence up the Ohio River, to the mouth of the Tennessee River, to the place of beginning.

ARTICLE 3. In consideration for the relinquishment of claim and cession of lands in the preceding article, and to perpetuate the happiness of the

The 1818 Treaty with the Chickasaw Indians   107

Chickasaw Nation of Indians, the Commissioners of the United States, before named, agree to allow the said nation the sum of twenty thousand dollars per annum, for fifteen successive years, to be paid annually, and as a further consideration for the objects aforesaid, and at the request of the chiefs of the said Indian nation, the Commissioners agree to pay Captain John Gordon, of Tennessee, the sum of one thousand one hundred and fifteen dollars, it being debt due by General William Colbert, of said nation, to the aforesaid Gordon, and the further sum of two thousand dollars, due by said nation of Indians, to Captain David Smith, now of Kentucky, for that sum by him expended, in supplying himself and forty soldiers from Tennessee, in the year one thousand seven hundred and ninety-five, when assisting them (at their request and invitation) in defending their towns against the invasion of the Creek Indians, both sums, (on the application of the said nation) is to be paid, within sixty days after ratification of third treaty, to the aforesaid Gordon and Smith.

ARTICLE 4. The Commissioners agree, on the further and particle application of the chiefs, and for the benefit of the poor and warriors of the said nation, that a tract of land, containing four miles square, to include a salt lick or springs, on or near the river Sandy, a branch of the Tennessee River, and within the land hereby ceded, be reserved, and be laid off in a square or oblong, so as to include the best timber, at the option of their beloved Chief Levi Colbert, and Major James Brown, or either of them, who are hereby made agents and trustees of the nation, to lease the said salt lick or springs, on the following express conditions, viz.: For the benefit of this reservation, as below recited, the trustees or agents are bound to lease the said reservation to some citizen or citizens of the United States, for a reasonable quantity of salt, to be paid annually to the said nation, for the use thereof, and that, from and after two years after the ratification of this treaty, no salt, made at this works to be erected on this reservation, shall be sold within the limits of the same for a higher price than one dollar per bushel of fifty pounds weight; on failure of which the lease shall be forfeited, and the reservation revert to the United States.

ARTICLE 5. The Commissioners agree, that there shall be paid to Oppassantubby, a principal of the Chickasaw Nation, within sixty days after the ratification of this treaty, the sum of five hundred dollars, as a full compensation for the reservation of two miles, on the north side of Tennessee River, secured to him and his heirs by the treaty held, with the said Chickasaw Nation, on the twentieth day of September 1816, and the further sum of twenty five-dollars to John Lewis, a half-breed for a saddle he lost in the service of the United States; and to show the regard the President of the United States has for the said Chickasaw Nation, at the request of the chiefs of the said nation, the Commissioners agree that the sum of one thousand and eight-nine dollars shall be paid to Maj. James

Appendix C

Colbert, interpreter, within the period stated in the first part of this article, it being the amount of a sum of money taken from his pocket, in the month of June 1816, at the theater in Baltimore. And the said Commissioners, as a further regard for the said nation, do agree that the reservations made to George Colbert and Levi Colbert, in the treaty held at the council house of said nation, on the twenty-sixth (twentieth) day of September 1816, the first to Col. George Colbert, on the north side of Tennessee River and those to Maj. Levi Colbert, on the east side of the Tombigby River, shall endure to the sole use of the said Col. George Colbert, and Maj. Levi Colbert, their heirs and assigns, forever, with their butts and bounds, as defined by said treaty, and agreeable to the marks and boundaries as laid off and marked by a surveyor of the United States, where that is the case, and where the reservations have not been laid off and marked by the surveyor of the United States, the same shall be done as soon after the ratification of this treaty as practicable, on the application of the reserves, or their legally appointed agent under them, and agreeable to the definition in the before recited treaty. This agreement is made on the following express conditions: that the said land, and those living on it, shall be subject to the laws of the United States, and all legal taxation that may be imposed on the land or citizens of the United States inhabiting the territory where said land is situate. The Commissioners further agree, that the reservation secured to John McCleish, on the north side of Tennessee River, by the before recited treaty, in consequence of his having been raised in the state of Tennessee, and marrying a white woman, shall ensure to the sole use of the said John McCleish, his heirs and assigns, forever, on the conditions attached to the lands of Col. George Colbert and Maj. Levi Colbert, in this article.

ARTICLE 6. The two contracting parties covenant and agree, that the line of the south boundary of the state of Tennessee, as described in the second article of this treaty, shall be ascertained and marked by the Commissioners appointed by the President of the United States, that the marks shall be bold the trees to be blazed on both sides of the line and the fore and aft trees marked U.S.; and that the Commissioners shall be attended by two persons, to be designated by the Chickasaw Nation, and the said nation shall have due and seasonable notice when said operation is to be commenced. It is further agreed by the Commissioners, that all improvements actually made by individuals of the Chickasaw Nation, which shall be found within the lands ceded by this treaty, that a fair and reasonable compensation shall be paid therefor; to the respective individuals having made or owned the same.

ARTICLE 7. In consideration for the friendly and conciliatory disposition evinced during the negotiations of this treaty, by the Chickasaw chiefs and warriors, but more particularly as a manifestation of the friendship

The 1818 Treaty with the Chickasaw Indians   109

and liberality of the President of the United States, the commissioners agree to give, on the ratification of this treaty to CHINNUBBY, King of the Chickasaw Nation, to TESSHUAMINGO, WILLIAM McGILVERY, ANPASSANTUBBY, SAMUEL SEELY, JAMES BROWN, LEVI COLBERT, ICKARYOUCUTTAHA, GEORGE PETTYGROVE, IMMARTARHARMICCO, Chickasaw chiefs, and to MALCULM McGEE, interpreter of this treaty, each, one hundred and fifty dollars in cash and to MAJOR WILLIAM GLOVER, COLONEL GEORGE COLBERT, HOYPOYEAHAUMMAR, IMMAUKLUSHARHOPOYEA, TUSHKAARHOPOYE, HOPOYEA-HAUMMAR, JUN. IMMAUKLUSHARHOPYEA, JAMES COLBERT, COWEAMARTHLAR, ILLACHOUWARHOPOYEA, military leaders, one hundred dollars each, and due further agree, that any annuity herefore secured to the Chickasaw Nation of Indians, by treaty, to be paid in goods, shall hereafter be paid in cash.

In testimony whereof the said Commissioners, and undersigned chiefs and warriors, have set their hands and seals. Done at the treaty ground east of Old Town, this nineteenth day of October, in the year of our Lord one thousand eight hundred and eighteen.

Isaac Shelby

Andrew Jackson

LEVI COLBERT (his X mark),

SAMUEL SEELY (his X mark),

CHINNUBBY- KING (his X mark),

TESHUAMINGO (his X mark),

WILLIAM McGILVERY (his X mark),

ARPASHEUSHTUBBY (his X mark),

JAMES BROWN (his X mark),

ICKARYAUCUTTAHA (his X mark),

GEORGE PETTYGROVE (his X mark),

IMMARTAHARMICO (his X mark),

MAJOR GENERAL WILLIAM COLBERT (his X mark),

MAJOR WILLIAM GLOVER (his X mark),

HOPAYAHAUMMAR (his X mark),

IMMOUKLUSHARHOPOYEA (his X mark),

JAMES COLBERT,

COWEMARTHLAR (his X mark),

ILLACKHANWARHOPOYES (his X mark),

COLONEL GEORGE COLBERT (his X mark).

Appendix C

In the presence of:

ROBERT BUTLER, adjutant-general and secretary

TH. J. SHERBURNE, agent for the Chickasaw Nation of Indians

MALCULM McGEE, interpreter (his X mark)

MARTIN COLBERT

J. C. BRONAUGH, assiatant inspector general S.D.

THOMAS A. SHELBY, Kentucky

R. K. CALL, captain U.S. Army

BENJAMIN SMITH, Kentucky

RICHARD I. EASTER, A.D. Q.M. General

M. B. WINCHESTER

W. B. LEWIS.

The Shelby Name

The treaty with the Chickasaw Nation of Indians was signed in 1818, ceding west **Tennessee** to the United States. The following year, on May 22, John Overton, James Winchester, and Andrew Jackson founded the city of Memphis. The county was named in honor of **Isaac Shelby** whose many attributes of honesty and bravery the Indians greatly admired.

Shelby County Kentucky was formed in 1792 and is located in the Outer Bluegrass region. Its county seat is Shelbyville, named to honor its first governor and hero of the Revolutionary War.

Other states have counties named in his honor too; there are nine in all:

Shelby County in Ohio was formed from Miami County in 1819 and was named for General Shelby. The population of Shelby County has grown from 2,141 at its inception to more than 44,000 today.

Missouri named its county in Isaac's honor on January 2, 1835. Its county seat is Shelbyville.

Shelby County in Alabama is located in the center of this oblong state and was created by the Alabama Territorial Legislature on 7 February 1818. It was formed on land ceded to the United States by the Creek Indians. The county seat is Columbiana.

Illinois, Indiana, Texas, and Iowa also have counties named in honor of **Isaac Shelby.**

Bibliography

American Heritage History of the American Revolution, The. Bruce Lancaster, Editor, 1971.

Battle of King's Mountain. Historical Statements. Prepared by the Historical Section of the Army War College, Carlisle Barracks, Pa., 1928.

Bissell, Richard. *New Light on 1776 and All That.* Boston and Toronto: Little Brown and Company, 1975.

Bittinger, Lucy F. *The Germans in Colonial Times.* Philadelphia: J. P. Lippencott Company, 1901. Reprint 1986, Heritage Books, Bowie, Maryland.

Brady, Cyrus Townsend. *American Fights and Fighters—Revolutionary 1776–1815.* Garden City, New York: Doubleday, Page and Company, 1913.

Brady, Cyrus Townsend, LL.D. *Border Fights and Fighters.* Garden City, New York: Doubleday, Page and Company, 1916.

Buchanan, John. *The Road to Guilford Courthouse.* New York: John Wiley and Sons, Inc., 1997.

Calloway, Colin G. *The American Revolution in Indian Country.* Cambridge University Press, 1995.

Commager, Henry Steele, and Richard B. Morris. *The Spirit of Seventy-six.* Bonanza Books, 1958.

Davis, Edward Graham. *Maryland and North Carolina in the Campaign of 1780–1781.* Maryland Historical Society fund publication, No. 33, 1893.

Depuy, R. Ernest, and Trevor N. *The Compact History of the Civil War.* New York: Hawthorn Books, Inc., 1963.

Derr, Mark. *The Frontiersman.* New York: William Morrow and Company, Inc., 1993.

Dykeman, Wilma. *With Fire and Sword.* Washington, D.C.: National Park Service, 1978.

111

112 *Bibliography*

Eckert, Allan W. *The Frontiersmen.* New York: Bantam Books, 1967.

Flexner, James Thomas. *Washington, the Indispensable Man.* New York: New American Library, 1969.

Fleming, Thomas J. *Year of Illusion—1776.* New York: Norton Publishing Co., 1975.

Gallaway, Howard S. *The Shelby Family—Ancestors and Descendants of John S. and his Son, David.* Mobile, Alabama: Gill Printing Company, 1964.

Hoxie, Frederick E. *Encyclopedia of North American Indians.* New York and Boston: Houghton Mifflin Company, 1996.

Hurt, R. Douglas. *The Ohio Frontier.* Bloomington and Indianapolis: Indiana University Press, 1996.

Hurwitz, Howard L. *An Encyclopedic Dictionary of American History.* New York: Washington Square Press, 1968.

Indian Warfare in Western Pennsylvania and Northwestern Virginia at the Time of the American Revolution. Edited by Jared C. Lobdell with notes by Lyman Copeland Draper. Published for the Draper Society by Heritage Books, Inc., Bowie, Maryland, 1992.

Kentucky Explorer, The. June 1992 edition. (200th anniversary of Kentucky.)

Lancaster, Bruce. *The American Heritage History of the American Revolution.* New York: American Heritage/Bonanza Books, 1971.

Lawson, Don. *The War of 1812.* New York, London and Toronto: Abelard-Schuman, 1966.

Marshall, John. *The Life of George Washington.* Vol. 3. The Citizen's Guild of Washington's Boyhood Home. Fredericksburg, Virginia, 1926.

McDowell, Bart. *The Revolutionary War.* The National Geographic Society, Washington, D.C., 1967.

Messick, Hank. *King's Mountain.* Boston and Toronto: Little Brown and Company, 1976.

Mitchell, Lt. Col. Joseph B. *Decisive Battles of the American Revolution.* Greenwich, Connecticut: Fawcett Publications, Inc., 1962.

Morris, Richard B. *The LIFE History of the United States—1775–1789.* Time/Life Books, 1963.

Pearson, Michael. *Those Damned Rebels.* New York: G. P. Putnam and Sons, 1972.

Rankin, High F. *The North Carolina Continentals.* Chapel Hill: The University of North Carolina Press, 1971.

Scheer, George F., and Hugh F. Rankin. *Rebels and Redcoats.* Cleveland and New York: World Publishing Company, 1957.

Selby, John. *The Road to Yorktown.* New York: St. Martin's Press, 1976.

Bibliography

Shelby, Cass. *The Shelby Family in America.* Chattanooga, Tennessee: Lookout Publishing Company, 1927.

Shelby Exchange, The. A quarterly publication collected and edited by Judith A. Trolinger, Hunt Star Route, Box 234, Ingram, Texas 78025-9704.

Ten plus volumes of genealogical research on the Shelby family and its descendants. Write for subscription rates.

Stember, Sol. *The Bicentennial Guide to the American Revolution.* Saturday Review Press. E. P. Dalton Company, 1976.

Sword, Gerald. *The Birthplace and Childhood Home of Isaac Shelby in Washington County, Maryland.* Prepared for Mr. John Frye, chairman of the Washington County Historical Advisory Committee, Hagerstown, Maryland, 1972.

———. *A Quest for Isaac Shelby in Washington County, Maryland.*

MMS. December 1971. The Western Maryland Room of the Washington County Free Library, Hagerstown, Maryland.

"Through Indian Eyes." Pleasantville, N.Y.: The Reader's Digest Association, Inc., 1995.

Wright, Esmond. *Washington and the American Revolution.* New York: Collier Books, 1962.

Wroble, Sylvia, and George Grider. *Isaac Shelby, Kentucky's First Governor.* Danville, Kentucky: Cumberland Press, 1973.

Index

(* Identifies a veteran of King's Mountain who served under Isaac Shelby's command.)

(# Identifies men who served in the Battle of Point Pleasant in the Fincastle, Virginia Militia Company commanded by Isaac Shelby's father Captain Evan Shelby, and in which Isaac also served as an officer.)

A

* Abernathy, Robert, 96
* Adair, John, 26, 96
* Adams, John, 95
* Allan, Moses, 96
* Allison, John, 96
Amherstburg, Canada, 81–82
Andre, Major John, 53
Armstrong, George, 103
Arnold, Benedict, 53

B

Bald of Roan Mountain, North Carolina, 28
* Beeler, Jacob, 96
* Beeler, Joseph, 96
* Bell, Samuel, 96
* Bell, Thomas, 97
Berkeley, Sir William (governor of Virginia), 5
Berry, Adam, 38
Berry, Andrew, 53
Blackburn, Arthur, 103
* Blackburn, Robert, 97
"Blue Hen's Chickens," 54
Bogard, Abram, 103
Boone, Daniel, 8, 25, 64, 70
Boone, Squire, 8
Boston, Massacre, viii
Boston Tea Party, viii
Bouquet, General Henry, 1
Bradley, John, 103
Breed's Hill, battle of, ix

* Brooks, George, 103
Bristol, Tennessee, 4
Bristol, Virginia, 4
Brown, Major James, 107
Brown's Creek, South Carolina, 13
Brown, John, 66
* Bruster, E., 97
Bryant's Station, Kentucky, 62
Buford, Colonel Abraham, 36
Bunker Hill, battle of (Breed's Hill), ix
Burck, Richard, 103
Burke County, North Carolina, 9
Butler, Adjutant General Robert, 110
Butler, Simon, 8

C

Call, Captain R. K. (USA), 110
Camden, South Carolina, vii, 21, 23
Campbell, Colonel William: Shelby seeks Campbell's help, 25–26; elected to command, 28–29; nearing King's Mountain, 32; hanging a Loyalist, 34; opening fire at King's Mountain, 38; reaching the top of King's Mountain, 41; report by one of his soldiers, 42; orders men to fire on Loyalists, 45; asks for casualty list, plans hangings, 49–50; returns home, 52; recognized in the North, 55; conflict over actions at King's Mountain, 94
Carmack, John, 103
Carver's Gap, North Carolina, 28

114

Index   115

* Carwell, Alexander, 97
* Carwell, John, 97
# Casey, William, 103
Caswell, Richard (governor of North Carolina), 21
Cedar Springs, South Carolina, second battle of, 13–14
Centre College, Danville, Kentucky, 92
* Chambers, Daniel, 97
* Chambers, Robert, 97
Chambers, Sam, 50
* Chaney, Thomas, 97
Charleston, South Carolina, vii, x, 23, 36
Chau-be-nee (aide to Tecumseh, also known as Coalburner), 81
Cherokee Ford, South Carolina, 30, 32
Cherokee Nation, ix
Chesney, Captain Alexander, 37
Chickamauga towns (Cherokee), 57, 60
Chickasaw Indian Nation, 92–93, 106–108, 110
Chief Anpassantubby (Chickasaw), 109
Chief Blue Jacket (Shawnee), 66
Chief (King) Chinnubby (Chickasaw), 109
Chief Cornstalk (Shawnee), 7
Chief Hoypoyeahaummar (Chickasaw), 109
Chief Ickaryoucuttaha (Chickasaw), 109
Chief Illachouwarhopoyea (Chickasaw), 109
Chief Immartarharmicco (Chickasaw), 109
Chief Immauklusharhopoyea (Chickasaw), 109
Chief Levi Colbert (Cherokee), 107, 109
Chief Little Turtle (Mishikinakwa, Miami war leader), 66
Chief Tecumseh (Shawnee), 73, 81–83, 87–88, 91
Chief Tesshuamingo (Chickasaw), 109
Chief Tushkaarhopoye (Chickasaw), 109
Chief Walk-in-Water (Wyandot), 82
* Christian, Gilbert, 97
Chronicle, Major William, 29, 34, 38, 40, 49
Clark, George Rogers, 8, 70
Clarke, Colonel Elijah, 9–11, 13–15, 19, 21–22
Clay, General Green, 76
Clay, Henry, 73, 90–91, 93
Clear Spring, Maryland, 1, 4
* Clemm, William, 97
Cleveland, Colonel Benjamin, 22, 28, 39, 41, 51, 54–55
Cleveland County, South Carolina, viii
* Cleveland, John, 97
Clinton, Major General Sir Henry, 46
Coalburner (aide to Tecumseh, also known as Chau-be-nee), 81
* Cobb, Arthur, 97
* Cobb, Pharoh, 97

* Cobb, William, Jr., 97
* Cobb, William, Sr., 97
* Cocke, William, 97
Colbert's Ferry, Colonel George (on the Tennessee River), 106
Colbert, Major James, 108
Colbert, General William, 107
* Collins, James, 42, 45, 48, 98
Common Sense, ix
Continental army, the, ix
Continental Congress, the First, ix, 53
Cooke, Captain William, 10–11
Cornwallis, Major General Lord Earl: ignores western Carolinas, viii; surrenders at Yorktown (in chronology), x; plans to end war, 23; Ferguson asks for his help, 29–31, 35; follows up on Charleston, South Carolina, victory, 36; at Charlotte, 40; receives report on King's Mountain, 42; army loses, blames others, 46–48; feared by Patriots, 52–54; gives orders to destroy Americans, battle of Cowpens, 56–59
Cowpens, South Carolina, x, 31, 56–57
Cox, Latitia, 1
* Cox, William, 98
Crab Orchard Springs, Kentucky, 63
Crawford, James, 50
Cresap, Captain Michael, 6
Crockett, Davy, 26
* Crockett, John, 8, 26, 98
Crockett, Joseph, 26
Crockett, Walter, 26
Crockett, William, 26
Crown Point, Canada, battle of, ix
Cruger, Colonel John Harris, 23
Culbertson, Joseph, 15
* Culbertson, Josiah, 98
Cumberland, Maryland, 7

D

* Daugherty, George, 98
* Dawson, Elias, 98
* Delaney, William, 98
dePeyster, Captain Abraham, 37, 42, 47, 51
* Detgaoorett, John, 98
Detroit, Michigan, 81
Dickert, John, 27
Doak, Reverend Samuel, 27–28
Downs, Mr. and Mrs. Charles, 4
Draper, Lyman C., 11
Dudley, Lieutenant Colonel William, 76
Dunmore, Lord John Murray (fourth earl of, governor of Virginia); predicts American revolution, 5; late for battle, 6;

Index

disbands valley militia, 8; county carries name of royal house, 64

E

Earl's Ford, battle of, 9
Edmondson, Captain William, 38, 104
Elliott, Isabella, 63
* Elliot, James, 98
Erwin, Hugh, 38, 53

F

* Fagan, John, 98
# Fain, John, 103
* Fapolson, John, 98
"Father of Kentucky," 94
Ferguson, Major Patrick: threatens Patriots, vii; poem of his defeat, xi; observed by Patriots, 13; at Cedar Springs, 15; at Fair Forest, 17–18; on Shelby's flank, 21–22; to eliminate "backwater men," message to Shelby, 24–26; avoids mountain men, settles on King's Mountain, 28–34; messenger identifies him to Shelby, 35; battle of King's Mountain, his death, 37–43; supplies captured, no help, 47–48; Patriots save Loyalist from gallows, 50–51; rumors of defeat and losses spread, 53–55; in Shelby's letter to his father, 104
Fiedler, Charles, 103
Fields, Colonel John, 7
Fincastle County, Virginia, 8
Findley, John, 103
* Fleming, John, 99
Fort Defiance, Ohio, 75
Fort Detroit, Canada, 74
Fort Duquesne, Pennsylvania, 1
Fort Frederick, Maryland, 1
Fort Malden, Canada, 81–82
Fort Meigs, Ohio, 76
Fort Ninety-Six, South Carolina, 18, 23, 29, 56–57
Fort Pitt, Pennsylvania, 1
Fort Shelby, Tennessee, 8
Fort Thicketty, South Carolina, battle of (also known as Fort Anderson), x, 10–11, 13,
"Franklin," proposed state of, 63,
Frederick County, Maryland, 7
Frenchtown, Canada, 75, 89
* Friggs (or Frigge), John, 99
* Friggs, Robert, 99

G

Gadsden, Christopher, vii
Gates, General Horatio, 21, 52–53, 56
Genet, Edmund, 70

Gilbert Town, North Carolina, 21, 28–29, 49–50, 53
Gilmer, Enoc, 32, 34, 38
Goff, Andrew, 103
Gordon, Captain John, 107
Graham, Colonel William, 13, 53
Grahum, Benjamin, 103
Grandfather Mountain, North Carolina, 28
Green Mountain Boys, ix
Greene, General Nathanael, x, 57–59
Greever, Phillip, 38
Guilford Court House, North Carolina, x, 57

H

Hammond, Captain Samuel, 17
Hampton, Colonel Andrew, 9–10, 50
Hampton, Noah, 50
Hanger, Major George, 46, 48
Hardin, General John, 66
Harlem Heights, New York, battle of, ix
Harmer, General Harry, 66
* Harmison, John, 99
Harrison, William Henry (governor of Indiana): gathers militia, 73; meets with Shelby, 74; sets out for Canada, 75; forces massacred, 76–78; Porter's victory on Lake Erie, 80; prepares for battle, 81–84; Proctor escapes, 87; burns Moraviantown, 88; loans horse to Shelby, 89; Congress votes medal, 90; takes credit for Tecumseh's death, 91; Shelby recommends for secretary of war, 92
Hart, Nathaniel, 62
Hart, Sarah Simpson (Isaac's mother-in-law), 63
Hart, Susannah (Mrs. Isaac Shelby), 62
* Harwood, William, 99
Henderson and Company, 8
Henderson, Judge Richard, 27
* Hendricks, David, 99
Henry, Governor Patrick, 5, 8
Henry, Robert, 38, 53
Hensley, Samuel, 103
Herndon, Colonel James, 22
Herndon, Major Joseph, 29
Herrel, Robert, 103
* Hickman, James, 99
* Hickman, Joel, 99
* Higgins, John, 99
Hill, Colonel William, 32
Holliway, Richard, 103
Holston River, Tennessee, 4
* Hudson, John, 99
* Hufacre, George, 99
Hughes, Lieutenant John, 45

Index 117

\# Hughey, Joseph, 103
Hull, General William, 74

I

Inman, Colonel Shadrack, 18–20, 22
Innes, Colonel Alexander, 18–19
Innes, Harry, 66
* Ireland, Hans, 99

J

* Jack, James, 99
Jackson, Andrew: reference to battle with Indians, vi; defeats Henry Clay for president, 91; hosts Shelby, 92; begins negotiations with Chickasaws, 93; writes treaty, 106–10
Jackson, Miss Nancy, 10
* Jarnigan, Thomas, 99
* Jarnigan, William, 99
Jefferson, Thomas, 9, 53, 70, 95
Jeffersonian Republican Party, 74
Jeffries, Captain Nathanael, 10
Jeffries, Mrs. Nathanael, 10
* Jennings, David, 99
* Johnson, Barnett, 99
* Johnson, James, 99
Johnson, Richard, 73
Johnson, Colonel Richard M., 80, 82–85, 87
Johnson, Dr. Uzal, 45
Jones, John Paul, ix
* Judd, John, 100
* Judd, Rowland, 100

K

* Karr (or Carr), Robert, 100
Kenton, Simon, 8, 66, 87–88
Kentucky Convention, 65, 67
Kentucky, country of, 8
Kentucky County, 64
Kentucky Gazette, 65, 67
Kentucky Society for the Promotion of Useful Arts, 64, 71, 92
Kerr, Joseph, 31
* Keys, James, 100
King George III, 5, 13, 35
King's Mountain, South Carolina, vi, viii, 11, 30–32, 34, 36, 47, 49
King's Mountain, ballad of, xi
King's Mountain, battle of: turn of the tide, vi; makeup of the armies, 29; the fight begins, 40; the battle, 42–46; British viewpoint, casualties, 48; news spreads, 52–55; Shelby's leadership questioned, 74; Shelby recognized for leadership, 79; Shelby's letter to his father, 104

* King, William, 100
King William American Regiment, the, 31
Knob Lick (Virginia, later Kentucky), 62, 64

L

La Fayette, General Marie-Joseph, vii
Lake Erie, battle of, 80
* Lane, Aquila, 100
* Lang, John, 100
* Latman, Joseph, 100
Lewis, Colonel Andrew, 6
Limestone, Kentucky (also known as Maysville), 89
Linville Mountain, North Carolina, 28
Little King's Mountain, South Carolina, 31
* Litton, Catel, 100
Logan, Benjamin, 8, 66, 70
Long Island, New York, battle of, ix
* Long, John, 100
* Long, William, 100
Lower Blue Licks, Kentucky, 62
Loyalists, vi

M

Madison, President James, 71, 75, 89, 92
Maiden's Choice, Maryland, 1
* Manor, Thomas, 100
Marion, General Francis, 59–60
Mason-Dixon Line, 1
Mason, Jeremiah, 4
Mathas, Drury, 38
\# Maxwell, Basil, 103
* Maxwell, George, 101
* Maxwell, Thomas, 101
Maysville, Kentucky (also known as Limestone), 89
* McAden, William, 100
McCall, Captain James, 17
* McClelland, John, 100
McDowell, Colonel Charles: asks for Shelby's help, at Fort Thicketty, 9–13; dispatches Shelby and Clarke, 17; leaves camp at Smith's Ford, moves to Gilbert Town, 21–22; scouts for Ferguson's location, named to command, 28–29; prepares for battle, 35; gains the high ground, 41; returns home, 52
McDowell, James (son-in-law of Isaac), 92
McDowell, Major Joseph, 52
McGee, Malcom, 110
McGilvery, William, 109
* McSpedden, William, 100
* Millon, ———, 101
Mills, Ambrose, 50

118   *Index*

Monck's Corner, South Carolina, 59
Monongahela, battle of the, ix
Monroe, President James, 71, 93, 106
Moore, Patrick, 10–11
Moore, Sam, 20
Moore, William, 45
Moraviantown, Canada, 83–84
Morgan, General Daniel, 54, 56–57
* Morgan, Isaac, 101
* Morgan, Thomas, 101
Morristown, New York, vii
Mungle, Daniel, 103
Musgrove's Ford, 17, 20
Musgrove's Mill, South Carolina, 17–18,
    21–22, 37, 47

N

Nave, Conrad, 103
* Nelson, William, 101
New Jersey Volunteers, 31
Newland, Abraham, 103
Newland, Isaac, 103
Ninety-Six, South Carolina, 12, 17, 20–21, 50

O

* # O'Gullion, Barney (or Barnett), 101, 103
* # O'Gullion, Hugh, 101, 103
"Old King's Mountain," 74, 79, 94
"Old King Shelby," 92

P

Paine, Thomas, ix
* Park, George, 101
Paul, Virginia, 47
Peach Orchard, South Carolina, battle of
    (also Silver Springs), 15
* Pemberton, Captain John, 101
* Penderegast, Garrett, 101
* Perkins, Elisha, 101
Perry, Master Commandant Oliver H., 76,
    80–82, 89
Phillips, Samuel, 24
* Pierce, James, 101
Point Pleasant, West Virginia, battle of, ix, 6
* Polson, Andrew, 101
* Prather, Charles, 101
Preston, Colonel William, 76
Price, Rees, 103
* Price, Samuel, 101
Proctor, General William, 6, 76–77, 80–82,
    84–85

Q

Quaker Meadows, North Carolina, 28–29,
    47, 52

Queen Charlotte (British ship), 80
Queen's Rangers, 31

R

Raisin River, 75–76, 82–83, 85, 89
* Reese, James, 101
Riggs, Samuel, 8
Riley, John, 103
Roan Mountain, North Carolina, 28
* Robertson, Major Charles, 102
# Robinson, Elijah, 103
# Robinson, Major James, 22
# Robison, Julias, 103
# Ruddle, George, 103
* Rutledge, George, 102

S

St. Clair, General Arthur, 66–67
St. Lawrence, Patrick, 103
Samples, Samuel, 103
Sanders, Hiram, 31
Sandwich, Canada, 89
Sapling Grove, Tennessee, 4
Saters, John, 103
* Sawyer, John, 102
Seely, Samuel, 109
Sevier, James, 26
Sevier, Colonel John: joins with Shelby, 9;
    alerted by Shelby, joins mountain men,
    25–26; takes position at King's
    Mountain, 35; Battle of King's Moun-
    tain, 41–42; saves James Crawford from
    gallows, marches home, 50–52;
    Cornwallis learns of his part in battle,
    54–55; readies for fight, 57; boxing in
    the British, 60; governor of Franklin, 63
Sevier, Joseph, 26
Sevier, Robert, 26
Sevier, Valentine, 26, 103
Sharp, Horatio (governor of Maryland), 1
Shaw, Henry, 103
Shelby, Alfred (Isaac's son), 94
Shelby, Catherine (Isaac's daughter), 94
Shelby County, Alabama, 110
Shelby County, Illinois, 110
Shelby County, Indiana, 110
Shelby County, Iowa, 110
Shelby County, Kentucky, 67, 71, 110
Shelby County, Missouri, 110
Shelby County, Ohio, 110
Shelby County, Texas, 110
Shelby, Major Evan, Jr. (Isaac's father), 1, 7,
    9, 63, 71, 104
Shelby, Major Evan, III (Isaac's brother), 26,
    58, 61, 70

Index   **119**

Shelby, Evan, Sr., 1

Shelby, Isaac: native of Washington County, (present day) Maryland, vi; wins Battle of Fort Thicketty (poem), x; place of birth, early years, 1; Lord Dunmore's War, 6–8; McDowell asks for help, 9; prepares assault on Fort Thicketty, the fort's surrender, 10–11; battle of the Peach Orchard, 15; attacks Ferguson at Musgrove's Mill, 17–22; organizes army to fight Ferguson, the march, 24–28; spy's report, 31; closing in, 32; calls war council, 34; deploys men, 35; attacks the mountain, 38–39; engages the enemy, 41–43; stops slaughter, 45; Shelby's report, 46; leaving battleground, 47; sets column in motion, 49–50; stops hangings, 51; takes prisoners to General Gates, 52; news reaches George Washington, 53; rumors reach Cornwallis, 54; victory credit to Shelby, 55; joins Morgan and Greene, 56–58; joins the "Swamp Fox," 59; rejoins Morgan, 60; surveying duties, 61; returns to Kentucky, 62; his father's antics, 63; builds home, 64; elected chairman of first Kentucky Convention, 65; names to Federal War Board, 66; leads raids on Indian villages, 67; begins first term as governor, 69; Indians kill his brother, 70; death of his father, farmer Shelby, 71–72; Kentucky politics, 74; orders troops to defend Illinois, 75; disaster at Frenchtown, 76; revenge, son believed lost in battle, 77–78; to lead men against Tecumseh, 79–80; takes position for attack, 82; discusses options with Harrison, 84; takes charge of prisoners, returns home, 88–89; Congress awards medal, 90; second term ends, 91; founder of Kentucky Bible Society, 92; negotiates treaty with Chickasaws, 93; suffers stroke, 93; the Campbell conflict, Isaac's death, 94–95; Fincastle Militia Roster, 103; letter to father, 104–5; Chickasaw treaty, 106–9

Shelby, Mrs. Isaac (Susannah Hart), 61–62, 92, 94

\# Shelby, James (Isaac's brother), 63, 103

Shelby, Major James (Isaac's oldest son), 63, 76–77

Shelby, John (Isaac's son), 94

Shelby, John Jr. (cousin of Isaac), 62

Shelby, Letitia (Isaac's daughter), 91

Shelby, Captain Moses, 26, 40, 57, 61, 70

Shelby, Nancy (Isaac's daughter), 92

Shelby, "Old Daddy," 74

Shelby, Sarah Simpson (Isaac's daughter), 63

Shelby, Susannah Hart (Isaac's daughter), 64, 92, 110

Shelby, Thomas Hart (Isaac's son), 64

Shelby's Wilderness Trail, 70

Shelbyville, Kentucky, 67

\# Shoat, Emanuel, 103

Slaughter, Gabriel, 73–74

Smith, Captain David, 107

Smith, Captain William, 9

* Snodgrass, James, 102

Society for the Promotion of Useful Arts, 71

Spartanburg County, South Carolina, 13

Stamp Act Riots, vii

\# Stewart, John, 103

Stone Mountain, North Carolina, 28

Stowe, Harriet Beecher, 71

Sullivan County, North Carolina, 26, 35

"Swamp Fox," 59. *See also* Marion, General Francis

Sycamore Shoals, North Carolina, 26

T

Tarleton, Lieutenant Colonel Sir Banastre: butchers Patriots at Waxhaws, 36; in Shelby's worries, 47; in sickbed, 48; obstacles, 52; orders from Cornwallis, 56; at Cowpens, 57

"Tarleton's Quarter," 37

\# Terrence, George, 103

Thames River, Canada, 81, 83, 91

Thatcher, Dr. James, 55

Tippecanoe, battle of, 73–74

"Tomahawk" rights, 64

\# Torney, Peter, 103

Tracey, Dr. and Mrs. James Wright, viii

Traveler's Rest, Kentucky, 64, 72, 92–94

\# Tucker, William, 103

U

Uncle Tom's Cabin, 71

Union County, South Carolina, 13

United Colonies of America, ix, 24

United States of America, ix, 24

V

Valley Forge, Pennsylvania, ix

Van Buren, President Martin, 88

\# Vance, Samuel, 103

W

* Wallace, Thomas, 102

Wasegoboah (brother-in-law to Tecumseh), 81

120   *Index*

Washington County, Maryland, vi, 1, 7
Washington, General George, vii, ix, 24, 53,
   58, 66, 70
Watson, Charles Stewart (son-in-law of
   Isaac), 91
Wayne, General Anthony, 70
Waxhaws, South Carolina, 36
* Webb, David, 102
* Webb, George, 102
* Wells, Joseph, 102
White Plains, New York, battle of, ix
Wilderness Trail, 62, 70
Wilkinson, General James, 65
Williams, Colonel James, 17, 22, 35, 40, 43,
   45, 55, 104
Williams, Jarrett, 103
Williams, John, 103
Williams, Mark, 103
Winchester, M. B., 110
Winston, Major Joseph, 22, 28, 35, 38–39, 52
Wofford's Iron Works, South Carolina,
   battle of, 14

Y

Yorktown, Virginia, vi
Young, Daniel, 43
Young, Robert, 42
Young, Thomas, 40, 43